Children of the Green

A true story of childhood in Bethnal Green 1922-1937

by Doris M. Bailey

illustrated by Jonathan Bailey

Stepney Books Publications

Acknowledgements

The publishers would like to express their thanks for the financial help granted by Tower Hamlets Arts Committee and Greater London Arts Association

First published 1981 by Stepney Books Publications
c/o 19 Tomlins Grove, Bow, London E3

Copyright © Doris M. Bailey

ISBN 0 9505241 4 X

Typeset in 10 pt Press Roman by
Printacolour, 101 Praed Street, W2
Printed in Great Britain by
Expression Printers Limited

To all my Dear Friends at 'Victoria Park'.

Victoria Park Baptist Chapel

We picked up the sheep droppings with a hair pin.

One

Defiantly, I put my arm around Tilly Goat's thin shoulders as we walked home from Olga Street school together that bright day, catching as I did so the queer smell that always seemed to hang about her, even when, as sometimes happened, she wore a clean dress.

It was a smell that used to pour out of some of the open front doors in our street, and always seemed tied up with children I was not supposed to play with. But today was different. Today, I had got a three. Now I could sit next to Tilly Goat, play with her and walk home with her. She was quite nice too, as long as you didn't get too near her. None of my other friends could play with me. I was now a three, and although inwardly I was dreadfully upset I could pretend I didn't care, and I watched Renee and Maudie and May walk past me on the opposite side of the road, put out my tongue at them and shrieked with laughter at something Tilly Goat had said.

Every few weeks, in those early 1920 days, Nitty Norah would come into our Bethnal Green school classroom. She was a thin and angular woman, hair scragged tightly into a bun, with a large round navy hat firmly pulled onto her head and a starched white nurse's uniform. Her lips were set in a continuous snarl and her nose twitched as though assailed by a permanent nasty smell. Come to think of it, she had a lousy job anyway. I never tried then to visualise her in her off duty time, but it couldn't have been all that pleasant for her. When other women talked about their jobs, she could hardly boast about being a "Nitty Norah". Even school nurse wasn't exactly glamorous in those days, festering sores and impetigo were too commonly their lot anyway; but the nit nurse, on an everlasting hunt for head lice, had the least enviable job of all. No wonder she was a sour creature. I wonder now whether she was glad or sorry if she didn't find anything all day. She must have been forerunner of today's traffic warden!

We would file out in silence and stand before her while the teacher sat beside her with a book. In one hand, Norah held a metal comb which she dipped into a dish of carbolic. She would lift our hair, peer at our scalps and then utter, one, two, or three in a sepulchral tone and the teacher would write it in her book. One, we were clean, two, she was suspicious of nits, and three, dreaded three, we had livestock on our heads!

After she had left the room, the names of the threes were called out, and these luckless ones had to sit alone in a separate block of desks. I had always felt a little pity for these unhappy girls. Some of them, in the dirty block for the first time, would sit and cry, especially as the teacher would warn the class not to play with them again, until they were dealt with. This meant that the nurse would come again shortly, and if they were still unclean, they would be sent to the cleansing station. They would come back from their afternoon trip with clean and shining hair, cut short if it had been long, and the dirty block would be abolished until next time around. Then we would all sit in blocks according to the monthly tests in the good old three 'R's, and I would sit smugly in the top place, month after month.

I could not believe my ears that morning, when the teacher called my name with the threes, after tight lipped Nitty Norah had gone. I knew I had one, I heard her say it; and I looked frantically round the classroom with swimming eyes. Yes, there she sat, another girl with the same surname as mine. She, who was always dirty, was sitting among the clean lambs, whilst I was to be cast out! I fought back my tears and tried to remonstrate, but the teacher only tutted. After all, in those days no pupil could possibly accuse her teacher of making a mistake. So I sat in the dirty block and shrank from everyone, trying hard not to cry. I was only seven at the time, but the memory of that morning has stayed with me all my life; for I learnt at that early age the impossibility of trying to reason with authority.

I crossed Grove Road and left Tilly Goat at the top of Hamilton Road. Later, the name was changed to Haverfield Road — the nearest we ever got to moving in my childhood! I took a deep breath, exchanging the smell of poverty for the lovely smell of new bread. On our street corner was a bakers, with the bakehouse running alongside. The wall was always warm, and stray dogs often sat there warming their thin bodies against it. Gangs of youths sat there too, playing cards, shuffling the greasy packs on the pavement. They had left school, but they were out of work and there was nothing much to do, so they played cards, or football. Our street, being a cul-de-sac, was a favourite place for games, and there were often fights when our own gangs turned on those from neighbouring streets and told them to get back where they belonged. An Englishman's home may be his castle, but the cockney fellow's street was his kingdom, and not lightly trampled on by outsiders. Even we small girls felt this bristling pride of belonging. I lived in the 'court', a narrow slip of a turning at the bottom of the street, and I can well remember shouting "Get out of our court," whenever children from the main street came down there to play. This was hardly fair on them, and a good job they didn't return the compliment, since we had to traverse their domain to get out of the street at all.

Past the bakers, the smell changed again, for next to the bakers was a dairy. No modern supermarket place this, for it was a real dairy with live cows, poor cockney cows that never saw a field. Often, when we went in with a jug for a penn'orth of milk, we would stand up on the stool by the open window where they served, and see the flanks of the cows and hear them softly mooing and stamping their feet. In the summer there were big sticky flypapers hanging up over the window, and sometimes they were so covered with flies that you couldn't see the flypaper at all. It was possible to buy new laid eggs there too, since they kept hens in the back, and when my mother sent me for a large brown egg for Dad's tea, I would carry it home carefully in my hand. We usually bought things as we wanted them, but I suppose eggs would have been difficult by the dozen, without egg boxes. Anyway, the brown new laid egg cost threeha'pence even then, so egg prices haven't changed so much over the years.

Every few mornings, the cows were let loose in the street as soon as it got light, while their stalls were scrubbed out. If they made a mess, it didn't matter in the slightest, because the women would come out of their houses with buckets and take the steaming dung in for their gardens. We didn't often get cow dung, living in the court at the bottom, but we had the advantage on funeral days, because the lovely black funeral horses always came down to the court to turn round, lifting their feet high into the air and snorting and foaming at the mouth. They were awesome creatures, in their black or purple velvet palls, with feathered plumes on their heads and their coats all shiny. Often, while they were waiting, they would lift their tails and drop horse roses. Mum always had a pail at the ready just inside the door on funeral days, and she, or one of us, would grab the pail and a shovel and scoop up the precious stuff before anyone else could get it. Old Mrs Kay who lived right on the corner had the advantage, but she was a fat woman, and slow with it, whereas my Mum was on the skinny side and much quicker. Besides, Mum had an added incentive, because a good load of horse roses would put Dad in a sweet temper for once, and that was always worth while. He would whistle softly as he shovelled it gently around our one and only rose bush, reserving a little for his lilies and carnations.

Dad was a real greenfingers, and this little plot of ours was his pride and joy. The place could not have been more than twenty five feet long, and he only had a four foot strip of soil along one side, but he grew a profusion of flowers all summer long and knew, not only every bud, but every petal he possessed. Every fish head was carefully buried near the rose bush, and when we had no manure he would sometimes send us to walk all the way to Hackney marshes, about three and a half miles away, armed with a small case and a couple of big hair pins. There we had to fill the case with sheep

7

Funeral horses provided the 'horse roses' for Dad's garden.

droppings, picking them up with the hair pins. We didn't like the job, but we liked the penny we got for the work. No royal garden was ever cared for so lovingly as ours.

On the day of the 'three' episode, I wandered slowly home, carrying my dread news and scratching my head because I had seen Tilly doing it. The front door was open and I yelled into the doorway:

"Mum, Nitty Norah came this morning and I've got a three!"

A sudden crash from the kitchen as Mum dropped what she was doing. "Three!" she shrieked, dashing up the passage and slamming the door. "Shut up, all the court'll hear you!" Not that they wouldn't know by now, with three of the girls in my class living in the court.

"You can't have three, you can't," she cried in distress. "Your Dad'll kill me." Wiping her red hands on her coarse apron, she began searching anxiously in the copper coloured silk of my short bob. Nevertheless, in spite of her negative search, she was taking no chances. The big black kettle was steaming on the fire hob as always, and she got out the lysol bottle. Dinner could wait. Soon my head was tingling and my scalp smarting with the fervent wash in piping hot lysol.

I sat watching her cook the dinner while my hair dried. She was a very good looking woman, my Mum. Not that I realised it then, but I often heard my Aunties say so. Bertha was standing right in the front row when the looks were given out. She had aristocratic features, big brown eyes and black curling hair which escaped from the tight bun at the back in little wispy tendrils. Perhaps her nose looked a bit large, but that was because she was thin. Her skin was pink and white, a very good flawless skin, apart from her work-roughened red hands. She was very energetic and moved like lightning, dashing through the chores and working with a will. She was lavish too, lavish with everything, so that our hand knitted dresses were always on the big side, our dinner plates were piled high and even our toothbrushes well endowed with the camphorated chalk with which we cleaned our teeth. Love and punishment were meted out on the same lavish scale, especially the wallopings! But they were quick hard smacks which she gave, and soon over, whereas Dad would prolong the agony, taking off his trouser belt, or taking the thin hooked cane from the wall and feeling it almost lovingly, prior to giving us a mighty swipe across the legs or the backside. That went on hurting for hours and I went on snivelling for as long as it hurt. My younger sister Gwen was made of sterner stuff: on one occasion, when the thin cane snapped across her bottom, she picked up the broken piece, handed it to Dad and announced, "Go on then, hit with two halves at once, you bugger." He was so surprised by the retaliation that he threw the broken cane into the fire and walked outside without a word.

I didn't go back to school that afternoon, one of the very rare occasions when I can recall staying off. Shortly before my father came home from work, I got another lysol wash, just to be on the safe side, and this was repeated daily all the week. Even now, the smell of carbolic makes my scalp tingle and the memory of that never to be forgotten episode is as scratch provoking now as ever.

Next day, Mum came up the school and demanded a recount. Clutching her leather shopping bag in one hand and her worn purse in the other, she bristled at the teacher and cast a few scathing remarks about those dirty old Clarks who spoilt our good name, looking across at Kitty Clark.

The teacher looked uncomfortable, it was the first brush she had had with Mum and she had probably realised by this time that it was unusual, to say the least, to see Kitty sat among the clean children.

Fortunately, Nitty Norah was still on the premises and I was marched into the boys' school by my angry protesting Mum. Norah grudgingly admitted I was clean — now. "No nits at all," she announced, after a thorough scratchy hunt. I wondered that there was any skin either!

Back in the class room, I was reinstated in my top place, and next time around saw the hapless Kitty back among the threes where she belonged. My sudden burst of friendship with Tilly Goat ended, but I always had a soft spot for her.

My main friendships were with the girls who lived in our court, Renee, Maud and May. Renee knew everything, except her tables maybe. She was nothing much to look at, being extremely cross eyed, but she wore steel rimmed glasses to counteract this, and every few minutes she twitched her nose to push the glasses back where they belonged. She hated helping with the household chores, and once out in the street, she would do anything to avoid going back indoors. Out of sight was out of mind, as far as she was concerned. So, when she wanted to spend a penny, she would jig and jig and cross her legs and dance about holding herself, rather than go indoors. There was a stale smell about her all the time; unlike Tilly Goat's poverty smell, but very unpleasant, and probably due to wet knickers most of the time. But she knew all the reasons for the street fights around, she could tell us why Mrs Thatcher had a black eye every week, and why Mr Green threw Maudie's handbag out of the bedroom window.

Maudie was a little devil. That was my mother's description. She'd come to no good, that was for sure. I wondered what coming to no good meant, but I shivered at the prospect. She was a beautiful child with bright red hair and when the sun glinted through the court and shone on her, it looked as though her head was afire. She made the most outrageous demands on her poor Mum; you could hear her screams throughout the court when she wanted a ha'penny and didn't get it. Poor Mrs Green would come along and borrow a penny for the gas sometimes, and we all knew it was to give to Maudie, because the screaming would stop as soon as she went back.

After her little brother was born, she was even worse. Then she stood watching the baby feed and would yell, "give us a drop." Her foolish mother would take the baby from the breast and hand over to Maudie, who would suck greedily for a few minutes and then spit out on the floor. Her father treated her exactly opposite. He was always threatening to kill her, and when she grew older, there were most terrible rows, night after night, as Maud stayed out with the boys and her Dad waited for her coming home. He'd throw her bag out of the window, take off his belt and give her a good walloping, but her soft mother would creep downstairs and recover her possessions and next evening give her a sixpence to go out with.

May was quiet and docile, always the peacemaker among us. It was May who would take the end of the skipping rope and turn it, May who was always last in a ball game, and she who would go and ask for our ball back if it bounced down the basement area of the houses at the end of the street. She was a thin plain girl with straight lank hair, and it's strange to me that I can remember her, seeing that there was nothing about her to remember. But perhaps she had lasting solid qualities that I sensed rather than saw, because I liked May, and was never happier than when playing shops or schools with her.

Two

How vividly I remember those Bethnal Green days! There were four children in our family. My sister Eva was six years older than me. Gwen came along just two years after me, and Rosie was three years younger than Gwen.

My mother's sister Lizzie lived next door, and she and Uncle Will had three children. Will, the eldest, was the same age as our Eva, Steve slightly older than I was and Jean a bit younger than Gwen. There was a gate between our two gardens and we did everything together, so that I looked upon the boys next door more as brothers than cousins.

My sister Eva said we lived in Bow. Indeed, our address was Bow, E.3, and it sounded a bit more posh, but whether she liked it or not, we came under Bethnal Green borough council, voted as residents there and had their dustmen and such like. But Eva would always strive to be posh. She was a pretty girl, very self-assured and argumentative, a fact which was always landing her in trouble. By the time I was in the main girls' school at seven, she had left to go to a Central School, a sort of half way house between the Elementary and the Secondary Grammar school. Children went there at eleven plus if they were reckoned to be really bright, but not brilliant enough to get the Junior County, which was the only means of getting to a grammar school without paying.

Eva had been in hospital with scarlet fever at the time of the scholarship, otherwise I expect she'd have made it, but anyway, the Central school was something and she learnt French and did algebra and chemistry. This last she really enjoyed and came home full of the experiments she performed. They sounded pretty gruesome to me, but everyone to their taste. I suppose she was a bit vain, but she was a nice looking girl, with slightly curly brown hair, lovely hazel eyes and petite features. She had nice hands too, and I well remember when she bought herself a bottle of nail varnish. It was colourless of course, but I couldn't keep my eyes off her shining, wet-look nails. I'd never seen anything like them before. When she was safely out one afternoon, I crept up and took the bottle from the box under her bed and painted my own nails. They looked so nice, but my joy was short lived. You can't hide your hands at mealtimes, and Eva suddenly spotted my shining finger ends.

"Thief," she mouthed at me, "thief." Even though she was mad at me she didn't give me away in front of Dad, which shows what a nice nature she really had at heart.

I shot upstairs after tea and scraped and scraped at my nice nails with scissors, finding it harder to take off the polish than to put it on. But scrape and scrape I did, though not without a pause between, while she punched me for stealing.

"Next time you pinch my stuff, I'll tell Dad, you bet your life I will, you fat lump of pud."

So I kept away from her goods after that, except for an occasional shake of her Yardley's talcum powder down my front, when she grew up a bit and started using such luxuries.

Sometimes, when she wanted to look extra nice, she would put her hair in rag curlers. The long strips of rag were wound round and round the damp hair and firmly knotted. How she slept in them I don't know, but the end result was a load of frizz to my mind, end being the operative word. I remember she once tried it out on me, but she might just as easily have spent her efforts on steel strands. I can still remember the pulling and tugging of those rags!

I've always had a good memory, in fact, I'm sure I can remember being born! The physcos would scoff at that idea, but I suffered badly from nightmares as a child. Whenever I had a cold, or childish upset, tall thin men in white would stand in the corners of the bedroom, and advance on me, swearing loudly and stretching out bony hands to grab me. I would run from them, run and run until I fell head first down a tiny, tight tunnel. This tunnel was slippery and slimy on all sides, and the slithery walls would press upon me until I felt I should be crushed. Then, just when I could stand no more, I would shoot out from the tunnel of horror into a huge, light open space, cold and echoing. I would start screaming then, loud piercing screams that brought my mother running to me. She would light the candle, give me a drink and sit on the bed awhile, showing me the familiar outlines of the room. But no sooner did she go back to bed, than the whole thing would start up again. This nightmare troubled me on and off for years. Every flu episode or bad cold brought the same sensations, until my own first baby was born. In a flash, it came to me that this was what my own nightmare was all about. It was just birth; and it has never once troubled me since. All very far-fetched I suppose, but it's a thought.

I can even recall sitting on my mother's lap during an air raid in the First World War, listening to pinging noises interspersed with bangs. Eva was crouched by her side, trembling and hiding her face in Mum's skirt. "It's alright, it's only shrapnel on the tin roof opposite," comforted Mum, but I sensed her fear and cried bitterly. As I was only two when the war ended, my mother was amazed when I told her about this episode, and remembered the occasion clearly.

I was supposed to be the brainy one of the family, but I have long since come to realise that cleverness in those days was merely having a good memory. I could look at a row of dates and know them, I learned my tables in the same effortless fashion, and it was easy to come out top in every exam when it was only a question of remembering which river flowed into which sea and how many half-crowns there were in a pound.

I learned poetry in the same parrot fashion, my favourite party piece being 'Young Lochinvar'. The family would stand me up on the table and I would begin, very soon finding them all convulsed with laughter. It was not a funny poem, but I ploughed my way through, never realising that it was my hopeless lisp which caused the amusement. 'Through all the wide borders, his steed was the best' was the line that really got them.

My lisp was never so apparent as when I had the misfortune to be in the class of Miss Griffiths: I defy anyone to say that quickly and often, and as all my sentences began "Please Mith Griffithth," I was always being laughed at.

No one ever suggested speech therapy in those days, and I suppose my lisp was completely ignored, because my school reports for those years show 90% or more for 'Reading'. Yet my present family get all steamed up and suggest sending my three year old grand-daughter to speech therapy classes, because she says she would like a "tup of toffee" and cannot manage her 'k'.

When I compare school today with those far off twenties, I shudder to think how the bright young lads and lasses of the present generation would fare. Sitting in serried rows of double desks, we never moved out of them except for the fifteen minutes play between ten thirty and ten forty five. Then we would queue up in silence and walk sedately to the playground, with a monitor on each landing of the stone staircase to make sure we did no more than breathe on the way down. We ate our sandwich, or whatever we had brought and went mad for about ten minutes in the small concrete yard. Then a quick trip to the outside lavs and into a silent line again for the return journey up the stairs. There was a big time-table on the wall, and we knew exactly what we would do each day. Every morning started with the singing out of the inevitable tables, but we knew them, they were seared for life on the grey matter of all but the most dim. We had never heard of a 'project' and in today's primary school, when I have asked a group of boistrous children, milling around the practical area of their school, what they are doing, it's always the same. "We are working on a project." If they are standing on the upturned tables, or throwing water and paint at each other, then they are 'doing a play'. No words to learn, nothing to plan and think out, no cues to look for, just 'doing a play'. Heaven help some of these misguided children when they set foot in the hard competitive world around them, when all they seem to know is projects and plays.

I started out left handed, but continuous raps on the knuckles soon cured me of that. Or did it? Even now, I'm cack'anded, to use my mother's expression. If I wind wool, I tend to put the ball round the wool instead of the wool round the ball, and drying dishes, I rub the dish across the cloth instead of the usual way round. But no one in our school was allowed to be left handed and that was that.

One day, I tried being funny. I put my mill board on my head and pulled a face. (The mill board was a stiff piece of compressed cardboard about one foot square, on which we rested our drawing paper during 'Art Lessons'). The teacher rounded on me. "Do that again," she said in a threatening voice. So I did, and how she walloped me! I went home sadder and wiser having had my first lesson in the duplicity of adults.

Our headmistress was a queer woman. She wore thick stockings with a draughtboard pattern on them in an age when everyone wore lisle for weekdays and silk on Sundays. Her tweed skirts were thick too, and her woollen jumpers tight across a buxom figure. Her hair was a mousy brown and scragged rather than pulled back and her glasses looked as though they had grown into her nose.

She would sweep into morning prayers and say "Good morning girls," with a terrific rolling of the 'r', to the four hundred or so tightly packed girls assembled before her. "Good morning Missawkins" we would chant in unison. Without a moment's hesitation, she would repeat the greeting. And we would reply as before. Sometimes, the whole performance would be repeated time and again, until we got the message and she was satisfied with our reply. "Good morning girrrls." "Good morning Miss...Hawkins."

I wonder now if she was a communist, or whether she belonged to some cranky way out sect, for even now, I remember the words of some of the hymns, of which we sang two every morning.

Hush, the loud cannons roar, the frantic warriors call,
Why should the earth be drenched with gore, are we not brothers all.
This was the one I hated most, it sent shivers down my back. One line 'sweet mercy melt the oppressor's heart, are we not brothers all' used to really get me and it was as much as I could do not to howl. Freedom was the keynote in her choice of hymn.

Men whose boast it is that ye come of fathers brave and free,

15

If there breathe on earth a slave, are ye truly free and brave?
In lighter vein was
   Life is a leaf of paper white, whereon each one of us may write,
   His word or two, and then comes night.
She was terribly fond of the brother theme, because we also sang
   Oh brother man, fold to thy heart thy brother.
I wasn't keen on all these brothers anyway. I didn't have any, and by jingo, I didn't want any either. If we had brothers and they grew up to be men, it would be like having more than one father in the house, and we didn't want that. One was plenty!

My father was a good Dad, as Dads go. He was a rather short, stocky man, with a little moustache and bushy eyebrows. His hair was thin, carefully brushed to one side to cover a balding patch, but what he missed out on his head grew well enough in other places. His arms were thickly covered and the black hair extended across the backs of his hands, and the thick hair on his chest sprouted even through his vest buttonholes. His fingers were long and sensitive, and he had a hatred of getting sticky. Funny this, because being a french polisher, they were always sticky. But he would never jam his own bread, or peel his own oranges, but hand them to Mum to do. He was powerfully built, and hardly ever used nutcrackers, breaking the nuts in his hands. He cut his finger and toe nails with a big pair of pincers, the same ones that he used to pull four inch nails out of wood!

He loved his work and many's the time I've watched him doing jobs at home. Spending hour after hour lovingly going over and over the same piece of wood, with little pads of wadding wrapped in linen and soaked in linseed oil. We had some nice pieces of furniture in our house, some of it acquired on a community type basis. My uncle next door was a cabinet maker. His boss would sometimes give him enough wood for three of an article, maybe a sideboard or a cabinet, and he would make up all three in his spare time. Dad would go and polish all three. The boss kept one and uncle and Dad had one each and all were satisfied with their bargain. A pity folk don't do this kind of thing more often.

Every Bank Holiday weekend, particularly at Easter, Dad would go out early to find extra work. Bank jobs were his speciality. What he meant then, and what young men mean these days by 'doing a bank job' are two very different things. When the banks in the city were closed, there was an opportunity for the long counters to be repolished. Rich mahogany, lovingly tended, not wiped over with a brush full of polyurethane as they are now. Dad took terrific pride in his work, and I still recall the names of some of the big London banks which he 'did' at Easter time.

All through the holiday he would work, including the Sunday, and then, when he got paid, he would take us out and buy us good new shoes. He had a mania for good shoes. Both he and Mum had bad feet, with corns and bunions and revolting callouses, and he was determined that we shouldn't suffer in the same way. So he would take us all up to 'Dolcis' near Liverpool Street, and pay about 12/11d a pair for our shoes in a day when there were plenty of shoes to be had for 7/6d.

He had this same spend-and-be-blowed attitude towards food. Sometimes he would stop in the Bethnal Green Road on the way home from work on Saturday afternoon, and buy smoked haddocks, or juicy kippers, or big rump steaks. No matter if Mum had already got the weekend food in. "Never a penny is wasted if it goes on your back in the way of good clothes, or into your stomach as good food." This was his motto, and we did eat well. A cooked midday dinner, something for tea, and when we were old enough to stay up for supper, there was a rabbit stew, or tripe and onions, or stewed eels for supper. Everything had to be of the best.

It had to be cooked well too and no fault was ever overlooked. If a potato dared to look black after cooking, and they sometimes did toward the end of the winter, then it was Mum's fault for buying cheap muck. A tomato had to be English and to skin easily, to be neither too firm or too soft, and if the bloater for his tea happened to look dark inside when he slit it open, then it was entirely Mum's fault and ought to be rammed down her throat. If he was not in a good mood, I'd watch with bated breath while he ran his knife along the backbone of the bloater and opened it. Yet he wouldn't allow her to serve it already opened. If my Mum had been given to prayer, then I think she would have prayed over every steak she cooked him, particularly on Saturday, when he had loitered at the pubs on the way home from work. If it was not tender enough for the knife to slip through like butter, then it might go straight across the room, or into the fire, or at my poor long suffering Mum. I once remember her spending the whole afternoon preparing a crab and making a delicious salad, because we were in the midst of a terrific heat wave and it was too hot to eat. When our lord and master came home, he asked in a very quiet voice what it was supposed to be.

"Why, your meal," answered Mum, equally quiet.

Then he let fly. "But where the bloody hell is my dinner?" he roared. The whole plateful went flying across the room, and the next half hour was given over to a tremendous outburst about a man slaving his guts out to provide money for grub, not bloody rabbit's food.

Rows in our house were the most one sided affairs. I often used to think that if only Mum had answered back and stood up to him occasionally, life might have been a bit different, for he was a real bully. But we didn't... we just let him roar. Many a night, my young sister and I lay in bed petrified, listening to the almighty din downstairs when someone or something had crossed his path and made him angry. Sometimes, Mum came running up the stairs and came in and sat quietly crying, on the end of our bed. We would pretend to be asleep and he would come belting up after her. He would open the bedroom door and point down the stairs. "Come down and take your medicine," he would say in a queer and level voice, and she would go sobbing down the stairs and the thumping began again.

"It's alright Gwen," I would whisper, trying to comfort my sister, "it's only because Mummy has to take some nasty medicine and doesn't want it." But I didn't believe it, and neither did Gwen.

"The old man was in a bloody temper last night, wasn't he?" Auntie Liz would say over the garden wall, next morning. "I wonder you're so daft as to stay with him. I'll be damned if I would."

"T'aint as easy as all that," muttered Mum to her sister, and then they would see me and shoo me away and they'd whisper together.

Of course, it was only the drink that got him like that. I often heard my uncle Will say that it was a pity that Joe didn't drink a bit more. Something would upset him at work, and instead of coming straight home as he usually did, he would call in at the pub and have a few drinks and brood on everything that had upset him. Then he'd come home and take it out on us, or my mother, if we were already in bed, and if he was late, then she'd make sure we were.

Normally, he came home every evening as the six o'clock hooter went at the nearby factory. He'd whistle a greeting as he came in the door, and we'd know, with an absolute certainty, that things were alright. If he didn't whistle as he came in, you could bet your bottom dollar that there was trouble ahead for someone, and we children learnt to make ourselves scarce if that particular barometer reading was not set fair.

Strange, how our timing was all governed by hooters before the days of radio. Everyone knew the time. There was the five to eight, the eight o'clock, two different sounds, and the same at one o'clock and six. Then there was the school bell. Early bell at twenty to, and late bell at ten to the hour.

Uncle was right about Dad though. Because at Christmas time, when he got really drunk, then he was very funny and he and uncle would sing all the latest ditties, and put their own words to them too.

You never knew how to take Dad, and it used to puzzle me. When uncle Will staggered home drunk on a Saturday, my auntie could get anything out of him. If we were around, and we'd always contrive to be, he'd pat us on the head, call us his little cock sparrer and give us pennies for sweets. If he was really drunk, he'd give us a whole sixpence, as like as not. We loved uncle Will. A kind and generous man, he was so easy going that he was the easiest man in the world to con. He would buy things for his two sons, things they couldn't really afford, and his little daughter could wheedle anything out of him.

Although I appreciated that drink mellowed my uncle, I grew up nevertheless with a deep rooted hatred of drunkenness, and vowed that I'd never marry a man who drank, although at that time I honestly didn't know any man who didn't. All my friends' fathers did, and so did my uncles. Drinking and pubs went with manhood and I knew no different.

Between times, my Dad was a good father to us, spending hours trying to help with our education, as he put it. This was my particular spot. He set me essays, and while the others were running about and playing games, I'd be sat writing, or looking up long words in the dictionary. He was proud of me and of my glowing school reports, and his aim was to see me 'go further' than he had had a chance to do. "I left school at eleven," he'd say, "but I'll be blowed if you are going to cut short your learning. I never had a chance, but you are going to get the Junior County and have a decent education." He taught us all to play draughts, offering us a penny if we beat him. I never realised how good he was at the game then, but since I have hardly ever found anyone to beat me at it, my tuition must have been excellent. Gwen was taught to box and fight. "Fists up," he would say, and they'd have a lovely scuffle. I sometimes think that she took the opportunity to give him a real hard one. Once she blacked his eye and he thought it was really funny.

It was one of his deepest sorrows that we were all girls. He was upset when Eva was born, annoyed when I turned up, furious that Mum dared do such a thing when Gwen arrived, and when little Rosie came along the aunties had to toss up as to who should tell him. He went out and got drunk and didn't set eyes on the baby for days. Had he been a Duke of King Henry himself, he couldn't have been madder at these daughters.

I was the plain one among the children. The only one inclined to fat, with straight hair and round red cheeks, big teeth and the hated lisp, I was nothing much to write home about. Dad loved me because I was bright and Mum because I was such a good tempered baby. She had had a hell of a life with Eva and I wonder if that was why there were six years between us. Eva, although a beauty, had been a real cross patch of a baby, and poor Mum, trying to undress the screaming bundle, would fumble and fumble until Dad came in. He'd take the baby, cut the clothes off it with a pair of

19

scissors and dump it in the cot, shutting poor Mum outside the room. There were endless rows about it, and I can just imagine how much Mum dreaded my arrival. But I turned up, fat and placid and smiling, sitting happily sucking my toes or fingers and troubling no one.

Gwennie, born just two years after me, was different again. She was a little five pounder, always small for her age, with a tiny heart shaped face, black tightly curling hair, and mischievous eyes that went into slits when she laughed. She was a little monkey, always ready for a joke or a dare and up to all sorts of tricks. She took after Mum and moved like quicksilver, and many's the time I've seen poor Mum chase her through the house and up the nearest lamppost. Gwen would shin up and sit cussing away on the cross bar, and no amount of threatening would get her down. She'd bargain with Mum though, and come down if she could miss the punishment she was being chased for in the first place.

Rosie was the baby of the whole family. Everyone loved her, a chubby little golden haired darling, too good for this world. I can remember her birth but always think of her as a smiler, never hearing the baby yell.

I wonder how today's Mums would cope with the washing and ironing of a baby in the early twenties. First and foremost of course, was the binder, a tight flannel stitched firmly around the baby's middle. Then the vests. Flannel one first and a pretty cambric one on top. Then, the long undergown, flannel again, coming a good eighteen inches below the baby's feet. This was folded over and pinned up to make a big bag over baby's feet. Then came the petticoat, gown and coat, followed of course by the big wrapping shawl and head shawl. Taking baby out meant a bigger more ornate woollen shawl on top of this lot, a bonnet and a veil. When I think that there were no such things as plastic pants either! The whole bundle could and very often did, get sopping wet through. This lasted for about three months, until the baby was shortened. What a relief this must have been for the poor little flannel wrapped parcel. Only then could the little dear show a leg to the world. But, boy or girl, it was dressed in petticoats and dresses and not 'breeched' until about two years, if male. Indeed, two years was being modern and I have photographs of my uncles standing dressed in dainty dresses at about four years old. Boys never wore long trousers until they were nearly fourteen and the first pair of 'long-uns' was always a great occasion. We were called to the fence to see cousin Will in his first long trousers, and felt him so grown up as to be shy of him.

But none of the delights of fathering sons fell to Dad, and what a blessing that probably was. I can just imagine a grown up brother dealing with Dad when he started losing his temper, so I reckon the good Lord knew what He was doing, when He made us all female.

Dad's one consolation, apart from his rose bush and lilies, was his pigeon loft. A tall, clean, well-painted structure at the bottom of the little garden, it housed about twenty pigeons. They kept him poor but happy, and kept me with permanently aching arms, since it was my job to get the seven pounds of pigeon food every week, as soon as I was old enough to go to the shops alone. No pigeon mixture this, as most men bought, but one pound of this and one pound of that, all mixed up in proportion by my father.

Every evening, when he came in from work, he would let the pigeons out for a fly round while he had his tea. Then he would sit on a little box in the garden and watch them, whistling them home when he thought they'd had enough. They were very tame and would perch on his hand or head and take food from him. Sometimes we got mad at them. Perhaps, on a Saturday, we had planned to go out somewhere, and Dad would let those wretched birds out for their fly first. This was all very well, but sometimes there were young birds out for the very first time, and they would be nervous, perch on the roof and refuse to come back to the loft. So Dad would whistle and encourage them, but it might take a couple of hours, while we stood and waited patiently dressed in our best, until all the birds were safely in. Only then would he rise from his box and get ready. Perhaps though, he would say it was too late to go out after all; and even if we were going to tea with relations and were expected, he would refuse to go. He never went out visiting in the rain either, if he could possibly avoid it. On many occasions, with us all dressed up and the aunts expecting us, he'd take off his collar and tie at the slightest hint of rain and refuse to go out. "No one will expect us in such weather," he'd say. Knowing him, no one ever expected us until they saw us anyway, for such was his contrary nature. I often wonder why my mother didn't just say, "Alright, blow you. Stay at home if you want to, but we're going." But she didn't. She meekly took off her best skirt, put on the everlasting overall and got us out of our best clothes. No wonder we didn't receive many invitations!

He kept a few fowls too, in our little back. No one called them chickens then, unless they were. But these nice fowls laid eggs, and scratched around in their little bit of dirt and enjoyed themselves. On one occasion though, Dad found that one of them had developed a taste for eggs, and was eating them as fast as they were laid. It didn't take the others long to realise that they were on to a good thing, and soon we were keeping hens and getting nothing from them. Dad kept watch, found the culprit, and gave her a good walloping with his leather belt. But she was too bird-brained to understand

Dad spent hours with his pigeons.

what the hiding was for, and apart from making me cry, it did not a scrap of good. Next, he made up a special egg. He filled a shell with mustard, pepper, pickling spice and peppermint. It made your eyes water to go near that egg. He put it in the nest and after one peck, all the hens were squawking around the run and shoving their beaks in the earth. But next day, they calmly went back to eating their good eggs. So Dad took the main culprit out and sold her, made a nesting box with a sloping false bottom, and all was at peace once more.

The cockerels were a different matter. Each year, we fattened two for Christmas. These hapless birds, usually Rhode Island Reds, were plied with food until they would eat no more. Then, Gwen and I took them into the kitchen, made numerous pellets of middlings and stuffed them with more food. I held the beak open and Gwen pushed the food down, until Dad came and felt them, and was satisfied that they could hold no more. Towards Christmas, they were kept in the house all night, lest they got stolen. Uncle Will came in to perform the killing (Dad couldn't bear to kill a pigeon). He would down a couple of pints first and then take the birds out and slit their throats over the dustbin. One year, we came unstuck. Uncle was unwell and unable to kill the birds, so a neighbour offered to do it for us. Dad was very grateful, until Mr Kay came along with the birds. "Thought I'd do you a favour Joe," he said, "got the missus to pluck and draw them while she was doing ours, so give me half a dollar and call it quits." He put the birds on the kitchen table and cleared off and for once, Dad was dumbstruck. The birds on the table were a couple of wizened skinny old things, not, by the greatest stretch of imagination, anything like our lovely fat cockerels. Dad was mad, but even he couldn't insist that they were not his birds. He went out and bought a turkey that year.

When today's children get bored watching the T.V. I recall vividly all our jobs. We had not time to get bored. There were a couple of rabbits in the back, and I kept white mice for good measure. Heaven help us if we let the rabbit hutch or mouse house get dirty. Why, we even used to polish our tortoise's shell with margarine, to keep him looking nice. We all loved animals and we had two cats and a dog besides. One day, one of the pigeons was ill. It couldn't eat, and Dad took it from the loft and felt it anxiously. There was something stuck in its crop which it couldn't pass. So he stunned it, held it firmly in his strong hands while my mother cut open the crop, removed the offending object and sewed the bird up with thread. Within a short time it was better and soon flying again.

To cull his flock was simple. A pigeon pie was Saturday dinner, and what a luscious meal it was. A whole bird apiece, the breast covered with fat bacon under the crisp pastry, roast potatoes and green veg, lashings of gravy and an apple tart to finish with.

Sometimes, if he was hard up, he would take some of the birds down Club Row and sell them on a Sunday morning. This was a glorious East End market at the top of Bethnal Green Road. No licences were needed, no permits, nothing at all. You just stood around with what you had to sell until you found a buyer. Once or twice, with Steve for moral support and a share of the spoils, I have gone there myself to sell a few mice for fourpence each. But I didn't like doing it much, because I was told that the man who bought them was going to sell them to a hospital for experiments. Dad had no qualms about selling the pigeons though. He had one favourite red bird, and every time he sold pigeons, he sold this particular one, as it would always be relied upon to come home within a few days! When we went out for the day on a Sunday school excursion or similar treat, we took the pigeon with us in a shopping bag and set it free as soon as we reached our destination. "Well," Dad would say with an air of satisfaction, "at least we know that they got there safely!"

"Thought I'd do you a favour Joe."

Three

The bakery and dairy were not the only places of industry in our street. Just past the dairy, there were houses on either side: one row with doors opening directly onto the pavement, and the others with a tiny forecourt. The latter were reckoned to be the posher ones, but the other side made up for their lack by whitening the paving stone immediately in front of the door. And woe betide any luckless kid who accidentally trod on a newly whitened doorstep. Half way down the street was a little shop. It was only a collection of sweets and small groceries kept in the front room of one of the houses, but we sometimes went there, more for the novelty than anything else. The woman was a sad faced creature who never seemed to smile, or even speak. She would slap down the toffee bar, or whatever we bought, and take our ha'penny with a big sniff. Mum always referred to her as the 'poor thing' but never spent anything there herself.

At the bottom of the street, where it met up with our court, was a fairly large factory complex, let to a gum makers and a feather factory. This was a queer mixture. The 'gummies' were a greasy looking lot, mostly men and very smelly when they passed us in the street. It was a smell like fish and soap together and I used to wonder how their families put up with it when they got home. But they were shadowy beings who just moved through the street twice a day, and we never got to know any of them at all. The women who worked in the feather place were grey: everything about them, coats, shoes and scarves, all grey, even their hair and eyelashes, when they came out from the factory. Sometimes when they were unloading a sack of feathers would burst, and if it was windy we would all get covered with feathers too, and my father would swear as he tried to brush his overcoat.

They made cushions and pillows there, and one night there was a terrific fire. What with the feathers and the gum, the flames were soon licking at every window. The firemen came into our house and stood leaning out of our bedroom window, to see whether they could tackle the blaze better that way. We were so excited, when wrapped in coats we were taken to a neighbour's house further along the road, all in the middle of the night. We didn't realise it ourselves, but Mum and Dad knew the danger. With an oil wharf opposite and a chemical factory next to the gummies, it could have been a dreadful conflagration.

But all was well, and next morning we clambered over the blackened ruins, together with all the children from the street, and looked for unburnt pieces of wood to take home.

There were three houses in the court before ours, but the house I liked best was the one directly next to us. A clay pipe maker lived there, and in his back garden was the kiln. The front room downstairs was the workshop, and we could look through the window and watch the old woman making pipes. She stamped out the bowls in a little machine and trimmed them by hand. Some were just plain clay pipes, but some had queer faces with weird expressions on them. She never looked up from her work, even when, during the hot weather, the window was open and our faces were only a few feet from her. She breathed heavily as she worked, and only paused to take swigs of beer from a big jug at her elbow.

Mr Hawkey, white faced, white haired and with a droopy clay-stuck moustache, would carry out the trays of made pipes to the kiln and stoke up with coke and wood. Sometimes it would smoke badly, belching out thick black smuts; and my father would swear like mad because his flowers were getting sooty. If it was a washing day, then my mother and auntie next door would swear too, but old 'Awkey pretended not to hear.

If he was in a good mood he would sometimes hand us a chipped pipe each, and we would race indoors and get soft soap from Mum and spend hours blowing bubbles. If no chips were forthcoming and we wanted to blow bubbles, we would pounce upon his dustbin and give it a good raking over before the dust-cart came.

Two doors past the pipemakers lived a little Jew who had a stall in the Roman Road. We could always call there for elastic or buttons or tape, or anything else we ran out of, in that line.

On the opposite side of the court were two houses knocked into one, where lived two brothers who were cabinet makers. Sometimes we sat on their window sill and watched them making chests of drawers, every bit made of solid mahogany and all the dovetailing done by hand. Dad used to say that they were real good workers and their furniture was fit to go anywhere. I often wonder where some of these chests might be even now, probably gracing some home where real quality is still appreciated. They were quite expensive, selling even then for as much as a fiver, but the men never seemed short of work. Sam, the older of the two, used to carry on about the slapdash youngsters of the day. "Never make good workmen of these good for nothing boys. They don't like real work and that's a fact." What he would have thought of today's lads I shudder to think. To Sam, a youngster had to slog all day and every day apart from Sunday, for six or seven bob a week, while he was learning the trade. But he would be taught real skill, though one wonders whether such skills would long be needed, in a world that was even then becoming machine minded.

When the chests were finished, they were covered with sacking and stood side by side on the narrow pavement, until one of the brothers tied them onto a barrow and wheeled them away. When the barrow was not in use they would let us ride up and down on it, although only the boys were strong enough to push it.

I could always rely on those kindly men for a bag of sawdust for the mouse house, although they did not appreciate my taking the mice over in my pocket to say thankyou.

Just around the corner was a house with an ever open door. Most of the women would trot across there sometime before dinner and place a bet. "Tanner each way," mostly...and how I longed to know what was meant by this. Surely, if the horse had to turn round and come back, and win each way, it would be harder for it than just reaching the winning post first. Mum didn't bet, and had scant sympathy for those who were always short of money and moaned about it, yet could always go over to Harts and put their tanner on a horse.

Dad used to have a flutter, but never locally. He always met a bookie's runner in Shoreditch, and if it was a very big race like the Derby, he would allow us to choose the horse we thought would win. If he took our advice, which he sometimes did, then he'd give us each a sixpence if the horse won. That didn't happen very often. Uncle Will always betted on one trainer's horses. At least I think it must have been a trainer, or a jockey, but in any case, every extra expenditure next door, be it clothing or outing, would be dependent on it. "Daddy says we'll have to see what Mr Cudby says on Saturday," Jean would tell us, when talking of a day at the seaside or a new pair of shoes.

Our main interests however, lay in the back of our house, rather than the happenings in the court. The Regent's Canal ran along the back of our garden, and many an hour we spent standing on the chicken shed watching the barges go past. Most of them were horse drawn, and did those horses get friendly! As soon as they spotted us sitting there, they would stop and wait while we ran indoors for a piece of stale bread or a carrot. They were lovely big strong horses, slow plodding and sure footed and they seemed to pull the heavy laden barges without any effort at all.

Most of all we enjoyed watching the 'monkey barges', narrow long boats gaily painted, with roses and decorative scrolls on the sides. They mostly went by in twos, powered by a chugging engine instead of a horse, and the slightest sound of their motors would send us dashing to the wall to watch them. They were clean and shining, with all the brass on them gleaming and glinting in the sunshine. Even their buckets, swinging on the sides, were gaily decorated with roses. Only the children on the barges looked dirty: poor, ill clad, scruffy-haired children mostly, and their dogs were lean and hungry looking. It seemed to me a most romantic way to live, but when I realised they were water gypsies and never went to school, I soon cooled off the idea. I loved school.

On the opposite bank of the canal was a big oil wharf. The heavily laden barges would come crawling in to the side and tie up, and the big crane would start its noisy clanking, picking up the barrels in twos and placing them neatly on the path. Then the men would roll them inside the corrugated red painted sheds, while the crane came clanking back for more.

Further along the canal, just within our line of vision as we sat on the wall, was a railway bridge and a goods yard. The L.N.E.R. trains came roaring past and occasionally there was a boat train. We'd wait ages to catch a glimpse of this, with 'Hook of Holland' painted on the side. My mind boggled at the idea of going so far. The goods trains clonked and clanked into the yard at the side of the main line, and the trucks would bang into each other, clink, clonk, clink clonk, klinkety klinketyclonk. At night, especially when the weather was wet and wintry, there was a strange comfort in lying in bed, listening to those fascinating sounds. They were friendly noises and the outside darkness far less scaring when I could hear the sounds I knew. I hated the dark and would put off going out to the lav at night, until I could persuade Gwen to come with me. Nothing frightened her, nothing and no-one.

My cousins next door were more venturesome than we were. On fine days they would slither over the wall and swim in the murky canal water, although it was too deep to stand in, even at the edge, and swimming was strictly forbidden. We sat on the wall on guard, watching for the water cops. These police patrolled the tow path, looking for trouble; and often the boys would have to shin naked up the wall because we'd spotted a water cop in the distance. When he reached us we'd say "Hello" politely to him, and Gwen would chatter on, hoping to keep his eye from the tell tale wet marks on the path and up the wall. As soon as he was out of sight the boys would be back again and in the water. They'd swim across and climb on the barges tied up there, and we'd sit and envy them. We used to worry our Mum to let us get down and paddle our feet in the water, but she wisely refused. Besides being dangerous, there was a six foot drop down the wall on the canal side, so we had to content ourselves with watching the boys.

There was tragedy too, in that canal. Sometimes, there was a suicide, and some poor devil, throwing himself off Green Street bridge, would come floating down. Other things floated down too, besides the flotsam and jetsam of the waterside community. Unwanted cats, newborn kittens and dogs that had to be got rid of in a hurry because there was a licence check. Seven and sixpence took some finding then.

I watched them drown a dog one day. It had bitten a little girl, and having no licence, they had to get rid of it, quick. They tied its legs together, poor whimpering mongrel, and put it in a sack with some heavy bricks. Then the sack was securely tied and heaved over the wall. We listened, dumbstruck, to the splash. Then the men who did it lit their cigarettes, went back to the pub 'up the top' and thought no more about it. Only I cried myself to sleep over that poor dead dog.

One morning Mum threw a rat over the wall. It was only a dead one that the cat had brought home, but it came flying back with a string of oaths, having hit a bargee fair and square as he passed by.

Dad had another use for the canal, besides using it as a rubbish tip. If we quarrelled over anything while we were playing, he would take it from us and send it flying into the canal. Ludo, Snakes and Ladders, dolls, books, you name it, we lost it, if we dared raise our voices in argument as we played. Only Dad was allowed to shout.

One day, a small boy was drowned there, having squeezed through a gate further along and fallen in, trying to catch tiddlers. We stood in silence as the ambulance backed through the gummies gate and the men came out carrying a little grey bundle. The women cried and the men doffed their caps, but Dad went straight into the garden and began looking out lengths of wood. He rigged up a narrow platform and laying us across it, he lost no time in teaching us to swim, working our arms and legs until we ached in every joint. At length, he proclaimed that we were now swimmers, and I boasted to all my friends at school that I could now swim. It was not until some considerable time later that I went for the first time to the public baths, and found to my dismay that swimming on dry land was an entirely different kettle of fish, to swimming in water. I shivered and trembled and slid slowly in, only to find that I sank as soon as I took my feet from the bottom. I went on sinking for years. Gwen had no such difficulty and was soon happily swimming around, and Dad boasted to everyone that he had taught her. It was some years later that I found out that Dad was no swimmer himself!

Uncle had better ideas about teaching his small fry to swim: he took his two boys over the wall and taught them in the water. But one Saturday afternoon he came home after the pubs shut, and boasted to his brother

Dad taught us to swim, laid out on a log in the back yard.

next door that his dog, as well as his kids, could swim like a fish. He took the dog over the wall, but the poor thing wasn't a bit keen, and as they struggled, kneeling at the water's edge, he lost his balance and fell in. What a struggle they had to get him out too! Auntie Liz though, was more worried over the fact that he still had his wages in his pocket than anything else, and she was through his jacket and had the pound notes pegged out on the line to dry, long before they were sure the poor man was still in the land of the living.

Unfortunately the tow path made a good getaway for thieves, and more than once we had all our hens stolen during the night. It was a queer sensation, to come down in the morning and see the fowl house door wide open and silence in the hen run. After the second loss Dad gave up keeping hens, but we were always very careful to lock the back door securely. Of course, Dad blamed the water gypsies, but he had to put the blame on someone.

There was a village air about our little court, for we were mostly related one way or the other, and most of the lodgers were distantly related too. Of course we had lodgers, I can't remember anyone in the whole street who didn't, but no one ever came round and said anything about overcrowding.

It was not until the big council estate at Dagenham began to take shape that officialdom started snooping around, and trying to persuade people to move out. In one house in the main part of the street lived two brothers, each with a wife and a whole horde of children: they had about eight apiece and it was difficult to remember which of the children belonged to which. One family had fourteen children, and when Gwen went there to tea, she told us that they all sat up the stairs with their plate of bread and jam. "It was lovely," she mused happily, "I wish we could have tea on the stairs."

We didn't reckon we were overcrowded, but in our little six roomed house lived our family, with four little girls, and Grandma and her three unmarried daughters.

We had the two main downstairs rooms, with a gas cooker installed in the back one, while Grandma and her family had the small end room. We both shared the scullery, with its sink, water and big old copper, but we had to go through their room to get to the scullery, and we carried all our water through. Of course, our dirty water had to be taken out in a pail, but we never thought anything of it.

We had the two back bedrooms, and Grandma and the three aunts had the big front room. They washed up there, carrying all the water upstairs and down again, but it wasn't convenient for them to wash downstairs, with us all coming and going through their place.

Auntie Rosie was the eldest of the three. She had golden hair and an exuberant happy nature. She laughed and sang, and enjoyed life to the full. She wore gold rimmed glasses and used lovely golden coloured hairpins to keep her bun in position. They were always falling out, and I used to hand them to her with great care, thinking they were made of real gold.

Lottie was only two years younger than Rosie, and they were great friends, going about together all the time. Lottie wore glasses too, but there the resemblance to Rosie ended. She had the most gorgeous chestnut hair, so long that, when it was unplaited and brushed out, she could actually sit on it. Her hair was more often made into two buns, one over either ear, but on Sundays, it was a big fat bun at the back. She was of a more serious nature than Rosie, but we children loved them both.

If we were ever spoilt at all, it was by these two aunties. I would stand at the corner of the court on summer evenings, watching for them turning the corner, then rush up the street to meet them. Rosie was a court dressmaker, employed by one of the exclusive Knightsbridge shops, and Lottie was a grocery assistant, also in Knightsbridge. They were both ardent Salvationists, and every Sunday saw them in their uniform, walking to Homerton, about four miles away.

May was the youngest of the three. She was a 'beader' and sewed thousands of tiny beads on lovely dresses, making intricate patterns on them. Sometimes she did home work, and we would sit and watch her. But not for long, because for some reason we used to torment her, and she'd jump up and chase us away. I suppose she was only about ten years older than Eva, and nearer to our generation, but whatever the reason, we used to get her rag out whenever we could. Yet she was very kind to us most of the time, and only threatened to tell Mum when we'd knocked over some beads, or made her lose her needle.

My Gran was adorable. For some unknown reason we called her Janet, although her name was Jane. She was tiny: so small in fact, that whereas I started out by measuring how high I came up on Janet, I was soon able to measure how far down Janet went on me! She was placid, perhaps the most placid woman I have ever met. She had left school at seven and could neither read nor write. Her mother had taken her to work with her in a box factory as soon as she left school, and sometimes the little Jane, standing on a stool because she couldn't reach the factory bench, would topple off, having fallen asleep over her work. She was a wonderful listener, and would sit with folded hands whenever we told her stories. Any story we had heard at school, we would run home and tell to our Janet. She used some real old fashioned expressions, and it amused us that she called scissors 'sithers'. She would ask us to 'run an arrant' for her, up to the nearby shops.

She had had ten children, five boys and five girls. All the five boys had died and the girls lived. "Very 'ard to rear, boys," she would say.

Sometimes, Mum would go shopping and leave Janet in charge. Whatever pranks we got up to, whatever we did, the answer was always the same to Mum's query. "Have the kids been good?" "As good as gold," would come the prompt answer, blindly ignoring the contents of her button box strewn on the floor, the overflowing sink in the scullery, or the splashes of red paint on her white cat!

She was very independent too, and although she came in and had tea with us every week day, she would carry in a tray with her own sugar condensed milk and bread and butter. Sometimes she would accept our jam, but not often. We fought to sit next to her at tea. I could always put my crusts, which I was not allowed to leave, in her apron pocket, and afterwards I'd watch her feeding them to the birds.

Her white hair was worn fluffed out in the front after she was washed and dressed, but in two tiny plaits across her forehead in the mornings. The back hair was worn in a bun all the time. It fascinated me to see her doing her hair. She would brush and brush it, then plait and plait until the end was no thicker than a mouse's tail. Selecting a hair from her shoulder, or from the brush, she'd wind it round and round the plait. When she'd put all the back hair into two plaits, she'd twist the two plaits together and pin it into the inevitable bun. Strangely enough, she never washed all her hair on the same day! Front hair washing day was far more frequent than back day, probably because the aunties helped her with this.

Mum had all her sisters nearby, with three of them in our house and auntie Liz next door. The lodgers in that house were an old aunt and uncle belonging to uncle Will, but they had only the one front room upstairs. Aunt Kate was an amazing old lady. She was known throughout the street as 'Mrs Dearie', because of her habit of calling everyone 'dearie'. She, like Janet, could not read or write, but she never let on about this. She'd sit holding a newspaper in front of her, listening as hard as she could to the talk around her. Then, "I see the papers say there's going to be another strike," she'd say, nodding her head. She also used 'face powder' and when she went out, made up 'to the nines' as Janet said, her face was white as chalk. It was only flour she used, but with a little bit of pink in each cheek and a jaunty hat and feather boa, she looked the lady when she went out.

She tried to play the lady at home too, and she must have been the cleanest woman that ever lived. Although she had only the one room, her home was her pride and joy. The big white bed covered with a snowy quilt, with white starched drapes around it and stiff white embroidered pillowcases, dominated the room, and draped across it was a beautiful neatly folded white nightgown. The bed always looked exactly the same, with its shiny brass knobs and dazzling whiteness and could easily have been used for a T.V. advertisement today. Just a snowy museum piece, was that bed.

When she invited us up to her room, we sat in awe on the very edge of a velvet covered chair, its white antimacassar tied with pink bows. Like a throne it was. Her cooking stove and washing basin lived outside on the landing, and she took her meals by the window, taking off the heavy red velvet tablecover to replace it with a hand crocheted table cloth and dainty china. She used to sing as she worked, in a very powerful voice that could be heard throughout the house. On Tuesdays, when she did her washing, she came downstairs and used her niece's kitchen, and then we'd hear her too. "Mona, I love you, Mona, Mona," she'd sing. On and on, so that if Dad was home he'd laugh and say, "Bloody old Mona's at it again."

Alas though, she had one dirty acquisition. An exceedingly filthy and scruffy little husband called George, who talked to himself and was always drunk. We used to stand outside the lav and listen to him, going on and on.

"That's it," he'd say. "Be a man. Nothing to it. Go up and demand. Demand. That's it. Demand. Don't go on being a silly bugger. Stand up."

We'd shake with laughter and mouth the words to each other. "Demand, be a man." I strongly suspect that he took these opportunities, sitting out there on the throne, to decide to assert his authority over his Kate, but it never came to anything.

On Saturday nights George usually fell down on the pavement, and aunt Kate would get uncle Will to help her haul him unceremoniously up the stairs. Not to bed however. "You don't think I'll have that dirty bugger in my bed, do you?" she'd shout indignantly. He had a little bed-chair in the corner of the room, covered with a serviceable brown hessian. I don't know how they managed, but according to my cousins, aunt Kate didn't sleep in the bed either.

I know she didn't use it for her afternoon nap, and the boys used to get mad at her because she slept in their room. "Aunt Kate's on our Willie's bed again," Steve would say, and we tried to think up ways to dislodge her. It was maddening not to be able to get the meccano set out from under the bed, or get the chessmen, just because of aunt Kate. So we formed a terrific plan. When Steve came and told us she had gone in for her nap, we trooped quickly to the garden. Mustering all the tin cans and old baths we could find, we stood quietly below the window. Steve had a watering can, and removing the rose, he put the spout to his lips. We waited a while, until we thought the old lady had dropped off, then we suddenly let rip with everything.

Steve in particular made a gorgeous noise with the watering can. Today's plastic ones can't hold a candle to the galvanised variety.

Aunt Kate threw up the window and bellowed at us. She didn't call us dearies then, but all the names she could lay her tongue to. When she paused for breath, my small sister spoke up, loud and clear.

"You shouldn't sleep on our Willie's bed, you old grey mare." It's a wonder the poor old dear didn't have a fit and fall from the window! We scattered and made ourselves scarce, while aunt Kate went to find our respective mothers.

Dad used to get annoyed with old George too. Perhaps he had spent hours trying to coax his young pigeons back into the loft when they had been out for the first time, and as sure as he managed to get them down as far as the roof, old George would come out into the garden and throw up his hands, making loud squealing noises. The birds would take off in a fright and George would wave his smelly old pipe at Dad.

"There you are Joe," He'd call out with great satisfaction, "that's got them flying for you again."

"Silly old sod," Dad would growl, spitting in George's direction.

It was the aunties and their not riding on the sabbath that made me first realise that prayers do get answered. I was about five years old, and they took me with them to the 'Hall' on Sunday. Attired in a new white dress made by auntie Rosie and carefully embroidered with rows of pink and blue featherstitching and french knots, new ankle strap patent shoes and short white socks. I was justly thrilled with my appearance and trotted along through Victoria Park and out into Hackney happily enough. But gradually, my fat little legs grew weary and the new shoes started to rub a blister on my heel. And we were not even there!

"Don't you ever get a tram home?" I asked, trying to keep up the pace.

"Only if it rains," answered Rosie, "because the rain spoils our bonnets and they are very expensive."

So when we arrived at last I sat gratefully on the long hard seat in the Hall, and while they all sang and shook their tambourines and clapped and made a joyful noise unto the Lord, I screwed up my eyes and prayed for rain. Rain, on a bright sunny morning, when the beams of dappled sunshine streamed in at the windows, making golden patterns on the floor and turning the captain's plain face to a golden glow.

"Only pray, believing," sang the captain, her voice wobbling with emotion. "Amen, Amen," came a deep booming voice behind me, so I covered my face and sat with bowed head as I saw the others doing.

"Just let it rain, dear God," I whispered, "let it pour hard."

The service went on and on, and suddenly I saw that the sun was no longer shining. Within a few minutes there was an almighty clap of thunder, and when at last the service ended, the rain was coming down in torrents! No walk home through the park for us — in fact one of the officers carried me to the tram stop — and we rode home in style! So God, that God they always went on about in the Hall, did listen, and did bother, even with kids with blisters on their heels.

What tremendous possibilities were now within my reach! That event was one of the biggest milestones in my life, and from then on I began to petition the Lord with all sorts.

Auntie Rosie used to bring home pieces of material, little scraps of velvet and silk, and try and teach us to sew. She would tell us whose dresses they were from. Lady So-and-So is having this for her daughter's coming out party. Lady This-or-That was being presented at Court in this silk. I took the pieces in my hand, and wondered hard about the Court. There must be lots of different courts. There was our court, but that was a poor narrow street, there was the police court and I'd heard that often enough, especially in rows in the street.

"I'll take you to court, so help me," the women would yell at each other when they had a fight. But for Lady So-an-So to wear a lovely silken gown to go to court didn't seem right somehow.

So I brooded on this while Gwen and I held our needles in sticky hot hands and did our best to make neat stitches. Gwen took to sewing like a duck to water, but as for me, 'dog's teeth', they called my neatest stitchery. I dressed my dolls by the simple method of cutting a hole in the centre of the material, pushing the doll's head through and tying a sash around the middle. Some of to-day's young things look as though their dresses are made by the same instant dress method. I must have been years before my time!

We had an absolutely fool proof method of sharing the bundle of pieces, when auntie Rosie brought them home. We'd spread them out on the table, and toss a coin. The winner would choose one piece, and the loser make second choice. But in case there should be an odd number of special pieces, second choice would also have third choice and number one would have the fourth piece. We always felt this more fair than taking turn about. We had the same 'fair' method for sharing an apple, an orange, or bar of chocolate. One of us would cut the thing in half and the other choose which piece she'd have. Never were apples or oranges cut more exactly in halves!

On the whole I was far more interested in the *Daily Mirror* which auntie brought home from work, than all the bits of silk and velvet. While I was only supposed to read the 'Pip Squeak and Wilfred' bit, I often managed quite a bit more before they took the paper away from me.

"No, Dods," they'd say gently, "nice little girls don't read things like that."

I could never understand why I couldn't read whatever I wanted to. I used to take books that people had loaned to Mum, and read them in the lav. A favourite haunt of mine, I still recall reading *Beyond Pardon, A Woman's Temptation* and any Bertha M. Clay books I could lay my hands on, seated on that scrubbed wooden throne in the back yard. I used to take *The Red Letter* and *Family Journal* out there too, tucked inside my petticoat.

Sometimes, I got so carried away that I stayed too long, and when I eventually came out, there would be a dose of licorice powder waiting for me, sure cure for constipation in our house.

When I see to-day's children picking up their mother's magazines and reading them, I sometimes shudder, for so much information is outspoken these days, when it was only vaguely hinted at then. 'How to reach a Climax' I saw in one well known magazine, lying in a classroom of seven year olds. It taught me a thing or two!

None of today's Mums seem to turn a hair when their small fry take up and read adult articles. Maybe in these days when so many children can't master the art, the parents are only too glad to see their offspring reading anything more than comic strips.

Sometimes, when Dad came home in a bad mood, I would steal away and sit by Janet's fire and get her to talk about the 'old days'. We never tired of hearing these fascinating tales, although my Mum was scathingly unromantic about them. Janet would tell how Joe, her six foot two Irish lover, would sit her upon the window sill to say goodnight, and how they would wander off into Epping Forest and dream up plans for a wonderful future. After they were married, Joe would go out and spend whole days dreaming beautiful designs for furniture, which were going to make their fortune when someone took them up. But she never told how he failed to provide his family with food, and how my Mum had screaming hysterics when faced with a cod's head for dinner for the fourth day running. "It was the eyes I couldn't stand," Mum would say. "It sat there on the plate glowering at us all, steaming and smelling."

When money ran out, the family used to run out too. "Doing a moonlight flit," they called it. Stealing away at night without paying the rent. Rooms were easy to find and sometimes it would be my Mum, Bertha, who found a new place for the family. You just had to take a vase, or something like that, and stand it on the mantlepiece, and that was the accepted deposit.

On one occasion, the family were in dire straits and moved into two small rooms. "Only room for two children," said the landlady. So Janet nodded and took the place, taking the two under school age children with her. The other three were let in after dark, with whispered admonitions to creep quietly. It was a hard life, but Janet never complained.

"Your father did his best," she would remonstrate mildly, when my Mum was leading off about him. "He couldn't help being off work for weeks at a time with asthma."

"No," replied Mum," but what about the time when he did a full week, after being away for weeks. How did the money go then?"

This was a story that Mum never tired of telling. Janet had sat for hours on the Saturday afternoon, awaiting the return of her loving spouse. Shawl round her thin shoulders and shopping bag at the ready, she was only too anxious to get out and buy some decent food.

At length he staggered home, smiling and beaming upon them all. "Janey," he slurred, "you're a good little wife to me. Never complain when things are hard, always ready to put up with the hard life." So saying, he kissed his tiny wife and handed her a little box. "I've bought you a present to celebrate. Good little wife you are."

The little box contained the most exquisite silver pocket watch, a lovely little timepiece with roses adorning its face.

"Oh, Joe, I've never had anything so lovely," breathed his wife. She wrapped it up reverently, after showing her daughters, and put it in her old brown bag. "And now Joe," she murmured, wrapping the old black shawl tightly round her, "can you let me have some money to get a bite for tomorrow. I thought maybe a nice bit of beef..."

"Money? Money?" interrupted the old man, sorrowfully. "Oh Janey, haven't I just given you a lovely present? I've spent my all on you, and now you ask for more! Janey, have you any idea of the value of that little watch?"

So Janet took the little watch straight to the pawn shop, and it was my mother, who had just started work at three and six a week, who finally redeemed it. It keeps good time now, even though my mother was eighty-seven when she died. My sister has it still.

"There was no R.O. in those days," said Mum darkly, "when you didn't have any money, you went without. And we went without frequently."

I don't think Mum approved of the R.O. man, although he was a frequent visitor in our street. It was years before I knew his real name was the Relieving Officer, but I knew him just as a man who called on the scruffy families and the out of work ones. The little shops along Grove Road all had a notice bearing the same legend. 'R.O. tickets taken here.' I saw these bits of paper handed over for bread and potatoes and meat, but we never had them. We paid with real money. Neither did we ever say "on the book," magic words that meant that the customer handed over neither money nor ticket.

Some of our shops had notices up though. 'Please do not ask for credit.' I wasn't sure what credit meant, but it seemed to me that lots of shops didn't sell it, because I often saw people come in and ask for something in a whisper, and the shopkeeper would shake his head and point to the notice, and the customer walked sadly away.

There was one pie shop in Green Street which had a framed verse hanging up.

Some people came and I did trust them,
I lost my money and their custom,
I'll not give credit any more,
So do not ask me, I implore.

There was a whole row of shops at the top of our street, starting with the bakers on the corner. I always enjoyed going for the bread. Every loaf was weighed before it was wrapped, on a shiny brass swinging scale, and very often, if it was just under the two pound, a make-weight was added. Sometimes this was a lovely piece of plaited crust, and I would hurry home and spread it thickly with margarine and yellow sugar. I'd sit on the doorstep and crunch it slowly, licking my fingers and enjoying every crumb. Only Dad had butter every day; we only had butter on Sundays or when we had visitors to tea. Occasionally, the make weight was a bun, yesterday's bake perhaps, but very acceptable. Sometimes, we would get a bun even if the weight was not short. At threepence halfpenny a loaf, bread was good value.

Next door to the bakers was a greengrocers. We didn't like them much, so we'd jump up and try to touch the blinds as we passed, just to make them mad. But we could always get bruised apples there, and a couple would only cost us a ha'penny. Sometimes I'd get one for nothing, when I went to get a 'penn'orth o' poterbs!' – the cockney name for a couple of carrots, onions and turnips for a stew.

The butcher was next, and time and again I went there for two separate halves of sausages. Never a single pound, although they were for our dinner. Two halves meant that the scale had to go down twice over, and often gave one more sausage than the pound would have given. My Mum was up to all the money saving tricks. On Saturday mornings we sometimes went there for a shoulder of lamb. "A nice lean one for about two and nine." If Mum wanted belly of pork then she'd go herself, because I didn't like to ask for belly, and besides, I might get one that was too fat. My cousin, faced with this awful problem, once asked for a piece of stomach of pork and got laughed at. But Mum didn't mind. "Want it scored?" the butcher would ask, and when Mum nodded, then he'd yell to the boy in the shop, "score this lady's belly Jim." Mum would laugh and take it all in good part, but I used to blush if I was with her.

After the butcher, the fishmonger, where I often stood patiently waiting for a soft roe bloater for Dad's tea. Squeeze, squeeze squeeze, the poor man would pick up all his bloaters one by one until he found a soft one. And all for threeha'pence.

On the corner of the next street was a small grocers, quaint even by our standards. Two spinsters ran it, thin grey women with sniffy noses. The shop was as clean as a new pin, and the scales which hung from ceiling height were polished so brightly that you could see your face in them. The butter sat on a white marble slab, and when you went in for a quarter, the lady would whack a small piece into shape with big wooden beaters.

It was an expensive shop and we didn't use it regularly, but it was useful for odd buys, or when the weather was really hot, when we would take a glass dish for the butter in case it melted by the time we got home. I'd never heard of a fridge, and the only ice box I knew belonged to the Italian man who stood on the corner of the street in summer, selling lovely lemon ice wafers for a ha'penny. Sometimes ice was delivered in big carts to the butcher and fishmonger, and the boys would try and steal pieces off the cart. We'd pick up a piece if it fell to the ground, but that wasn't often.

Across the next street was the inevitable pawnshop on the corner, and every Monday morning there was a little bunch of women with a bundle each, patiently waiting for the shop to open. They mostly laughed too, "Just waiting for me wardrobe to open," they'd call, for they would redeem their husband's suit every Saturday and take it back again on the Monday. There were some people though, who slipped into the pawnshop quickly and shamefacedly: these were the ones who were getting pretty desperate and needed money quickly. I used to look in the window at the pretty rings and watches, but never set foot inside. Mum was scathing about women who always went to the pawn.

Next door to the pawn, was a sweet shop and tobacconist. I was more often in there for a twopenny packet of woodbines or the sixpenny packet of goldflake for Dad, than for anything else, because I knew a shop in Green Street where sweets could be had for a penny a quarter, and it was well worth the long walk to save money like that. Gwen and I would share a whole quarter sometimes.

Another grocer, where the old man would take about five minutes to slice two ounces of 'corn beef' and another five minutes to wrap it, and then a clock and watch shop and an estate agents completed the next row of shops.

Further along still were other shops, including the post office, the chemist and the oil shop. The last named I dreaded, for rumour had it that the woman there was a witch, and I was dead scared. She always wore a shapeless bowl-like hat pulled well down over her eyes, and she had to peer up under the brim to look at you. Her hands were grimy and smelt of the paraffin and her nose dripped continually. Her coarse apron was always grubby and I loathed going in, though of course we had to have a new mantle sometimes for the gas.

"Dad says will you please make sure it isn't broken," I would whisper, wishing with all my heart that I hadn't to stay while she took the fragile mantle out of its box and put it back again before wrapping it. "And don't break it on the way home," she'd snap, handing it to me with a sniff.

I hated buying paraffin, or a pint of vinegar, but it wasn't quite so bad when I went there with a basin for three penn'orth of jam, or two penn'orth of black treacle. Then I could walk back slowly, sticking my finger in the basin and having a few licks as I walked. These errands were mostly for neighbours though, because Mum bought our jam and treacle in tins or jars. Dad wouldn't eat oil shop jam, anyway, because he said he could taste the paraffin in it.

The chemist was a delight. It was no ordinary shop, being owned by a manufacturing chemist who had his factory next door to the feather factory. Most of his stuff was sold under quaint names, or formula numbers. There was a lovely one for children's coughs and it was worth getting a cough to have a bottle. Another one was very good for colds, and Dad swore by this one and was never without it. When the bottle was empty, he would use it for polish, as he did all the empties.

One day, he was sent by his firm on an outdoor job, that is, to repolish a surface in a private house; and he came into the room to find the lady of the house delving into his little black case of bottles. She looked up guiltily and said, "Well, polisher, you've made such a good job of my table that I'm taking down the name and address and formula number of the magic liquid you've used. I shall get myself a bottle and do my own repolishing in future."

Dad came home in a high good humour that night. "Silly old cow," he chortled, "I'd like to see the mess that cold mixture will make of her furniture."

He disliked intensely the 'jumped up newly rich' he visited. They never offered him a cuppa, and he might have walked two or three miles from the nearest station. There were no cafes around these new housing estates and he might have to go all day without a drink. But if they were decent and offered him a drink, or a bite to eat at mealtimes, then he'd do little extra jobs, or give them a drop of linseed oil and polish.

There was another shop I hated almost as much as the oil shop. This was the 'orf licence' and I was often asked to go there by the pipemakers, who must have drunk an awful lot. Almost every day, Mrs 'Awkey would come to the street door and stand swaying in the passage until she could catch an unwary child to send up the 'orf licence'. The reasons we hated going were threefold. First, it was a fair distance away and across the main road, secondly, the jug was a heavy old thing and hard to carry home without spilling, and thirdly, she was a rotton payer. Rarely more than a ha'penny, even if we had both a jug and a bottle to carry, and sometimes it was just a "see you later on" and nothing more. So when we saw that big fat swaying tummy appear round the doorway, even before we saw the head, we made ouselves scarce. She had a habit of nodding too, nod nod nod, with her arms folded in her apron and her bag at her feet, waiting to catch someone, while we huddled quietly in a doorway and waited for the danger to pass.

Her own two daughters worked hard, they were always doing something about the house, singing as they worked. They were both very musical, it amazes me that they never had a piano lesson, yet they could both play all the latest tunes, singing in lovely tuneful strong voices. Those two could have made a fortune with a pop group in these days. One was called Hilda, but I never knew that until I met her in school. With Hawkey as a surname, it was a poor choice. 'Ildrawkey' was her name, as far as we were concerned. Her mother called her Illy.

On the opposite side of the main road, was a big pub and I never knew it by any other name than the 'Vic'. "Up the Vic" was the usual answer of the children when asked where their mother was. Most of these 'Vic' women wore their husband's old cloth cap by day, with an old coat or jacket slung round their shoulders, or a black shawl if they were old. They would leave off work, even on washing day, as soon as the pub opened in the morning, and pop up the 'top' for a quick drink. Sometimes they were still sitting there yarning when the children came home from school at dinner time. Then they'd rush home and give the kids broken biscuits or an egg for their dinner because there wasn't time to cook anything decent.

Mum never went alone to a pub and was sharp tongued about those who did, but we always went up to the Vic to see them all set out on their yearly outing. They were already laughing and shouting rude things even before the charabanc set off for Southend, but they didn't wear cloth caps and coarse aprons then. "Done up to the nines," Mum would say. As they set off they would throw ha'pennies out to the gathered children, and everyone would scramble for them, but this practice was stopped after several children got injured diving under horses hoofs and bikes for the money.

Gwen and I had other means of making a penny too. My choice was baby minding and I'd take anyone's baby out, up and down the street for hours and, when I got a bit older, to Victoria Park for a whole morning. I used to love doing this, especially if it was a nice clean baby in a posh pram. I'd pretend I was a nursemaid, and I'd walk sedately behind a couple of real nursemaids in the park, until at last they began to talk to me. I really fancied myself then, for they wore uniforms and talked of their employers as madam. I thought how wonderful it would be to be a nursemaid, and always have a posh pram with silk covers and sun canopies. What bliss to spend a whole morning in such company. And then, when I got home I'd get a penny, or even a silver threepenny bit, for having enjoyed myself!

Gwen wasn't so keen on the babies. She took in mangling! We had a big heavy wringer in the scullery, and Gwen would call and collect washing, ready folded, from several of the neighbours, and put it all through our mangle. Once for thin things and twice for the thick ones. A hefty task for a little shrimp of about eight years, but she'd earn two or three pennies in this way, and it would save the women hours of ironing.

Occasionally, we'd collect up all the empty jam jars and take them up to the grocers in Green Street. About half an hour's walk this, but you could only take jars back to the shop where they came from. A farthing on each pound jar, and a ha'penny on a two pound one. It was a heavy struggle to take a bob's worth of jars back, but well worth the trouble, especially before excursion days.

There were two excursion days in our young lives. One was the Sunday School excursion, either to Southend or to Loughton, and the other the Band of Hope, always to Southend. These two days, and perhaps an occasional one day a year with our parents, made up the whole of our summer holiday by the sea.

The Band of Hope was held at the Lycett Methodist Church in the Mile End Road, nearly two miles from our home. But we went to the Lycett every week, and signed the pledge every week, too!

At seven o'clock on one Saturday morning a year, we were marched to Stepney Station, five or six hundred of us, and taken to Southend for the day. I was always so relieved to get onto the train. There was a notice just inside the station which read: 'Loiterers will be treated as tresspassers', and it was this which scared me stiff. For even the Lord's Prayer knew about this awful notice, and every week at Sunday School, and every morning in day school, we all prayed: "Lead us not into Stepney Station," right in the middle of the Lord's Prayer. So it was very important not to stop there a minute longer than was necessary. What might not happen, if you were unfortunate enough to have to wait there for a train and get accused of loitering!

I loved Southend! When we went on the excursion, we prayed and prayed for a fine day, and usually got it too. With a whole shilling to spend we were millionaires for the day: we could buy a plate of cockles and have an icecream and a 'go on the mat' (a big helter skelter outside the Kursaal) and even a threepenny boat ride. We paddled and built sandcastles and crammed all our bliss into one day.

Once, watching a poor bloke playing an accordion and not collecting much for his efforts on the beach, Gwen and Jean started dancing, a pretty little dance they had learnt at school. People stopped to watch then and not to be outdone, I joined in with my hopeless voice and sang. 'There's a blue ridge round my heart Virginia' I warbled, all out of tune, but powerful. And soon the pennies started pouring into the hat and the onlookers clapped the dancing.

The bloke was delighted, gave us a penny each and asked us if we'd like to come up the beach a bit further with him. But we had to decline, as we were soon off to tea.

Tea wasn't much. Just the usual bread and jam sandwiches and plain or fruit cake to follow, but as we'd spent all our money and eaten all our sandwiches, we were glad enough to eat up every crumb.

Then home we went on the train, everyone accounted for and nothing worse than a scorched neck or a grazed knee between the whole party. Rock for Mum and Dad and Eva and jelly sweets for Janet. What a day!

In some ways, it was even more exciting on the rare occasions when Mum and Dad took us. This time, we would get up early on a Sunday morning and walk to Bow Station, for there was a cheap trip from there. The platform was solid with people, long before the train steamed in from Fenchurch Street, and I used to pray like mad that we wouldn't be standing by train bumpers or a guard's van when it stopped. We would shove and push our way in, almost as solid a mass as the tube of today in rush hour, and as long as we had one seat for Mum, we'd be glad. There would be children on the racks and all over the floor and on everyone's laps, but for two and nine pence, it was worth a bit of discomfort. Once there, we would stream down the High Street, just as we did with the Band of Hope, but once we reached the front, things would be different. We would make straight for one of the big pubs, probably the 'Ivy House' for they had a sort of gallery in the yard, lined with trestles and benches. There we would sit and eat our bread and cheese and tomatoes, and Mum would cut us thick pieces of cucumber, while Dad went down to get a couple of pints. Then we'd enjoy all the excitement down below, where the firm's outings would be gathered in full force, wearing saucy hats and dancing 'Knees up Mother Brown', showing their knickers, and singing 'Bye Bye Blackbird'. They'd be drunk of course, but safely up there in the balcony, we'd be out of harm's way and could laugh at all the fun.

After Dad had downed a couple of pints, we'd leave the excitement of the pub and go to the beach. Until afternoon closing time, Dad would keep on taking a trip, while Mum sat leaning against a breakwater, keeping an eye on us while we paddled. All too soon, the wonderful day would end and packed tightly in the train, clutching a straw bag of oysters and a jarful of cockles in vinegar, we would journey happily home and wait patiently for another year.

Mum used to talk hopefully about spending a whole week in this haven of perfection, but Dad had no paid holiday and could never afford to save a whole week's wages. He never felt aggrieved about working fifty two weeks a year, he was just grateful for having the work. So we made the most of our day and spent the rest of our school holidays in Victoria Park with just a couple of trips to Loughton.

Loughton! What joyous memories we had of Epping Forest. Dad loved it too: he knew all the main footpaths, all the birds and trees, and a walk there with him was an education in itself. Besides, there were no pubs in the forest, which added to its attraction for me, and it was not until we had walked the three or four miles or so to the 'Wake Arms' from Loughton, that Dad took of liquid refreshment. But he never drank too much there. He was himself, a truly happy man, among the trees and the birds. We even saw deer there sometimes, when we sat quiet and still. Dad would fill all his pockets, and ours too, with the soft brown leaf mould, and carry it home and put it reverently around his rose bush.

If only we had been able to live there, his life, and ours in consequence, would have been so different. He whistled as he walked, he didn't smoke his endless cigarettes and he didn't even swear. He was in heaven and forgot all his troubles and perplexities.

When Loughton first started building semis, Mum had a wild dream of going there to live. She even saved the ten pounds deposit once, and found a builder who would pay all our moving expenses if we'd buy one of his houses.

As an added attraction, we could have five pounds rebate off the cost of the house if we undertook the scrubbing out and cleaning up of the new house. So glad were they of buyers of new houses in those days. But never would Dad sign on the dotted line. "All that debt," he would roar. "Me, buy a house and get into debt for five hundred pounds! Me, who never bought anything at all on the never never! You must be mad!"

In vain Mum pointed out fearfully that the repayments would not be any more than we paid in rent, but there was no moving my father and we never got to live in Loughton.

The Sunday School took us there once a year, but this outing was a much more select affair than the Lycett treat. There were plenty of teachers to control the children and there were no rough elements such as we met up with at the Band of Hope. We took a big ball and played games together, and although we enjoyed it the whole thing lacked the excitement of the Southend 'do'.

Funnily enough, although I loved day school, I was very loath to join the Sunday School. My older sister started going at about eleven, and after a few weeks she took my two younger sisters with her, where they loved being in the Infant department. Mum certainly encouraged this, although Gwen would sometimes stuff the knuckle bone from the shoulder of lamb in her pocket, to eat when she got there.

Thinking back, those lonely Sunday afternoons were among the highlights of my week. No sisters to interfere or quarrel with, and the undivided attention of the aunties or Janet, if they happened to be about. No one chivvied me about staying at home as long as I played quietly, until the sad day when Steve gave me one of his tiddlers after a fishing trip over the canal wall. I was delighted; put the fish in a jam jar and ran with it into the house. No one around – my parents having gone up to bed for their afternoon nap. I dashed up the stairs, barging straight into their bedroom with my tiddler, my face beaming with pleasure.

Dad let out a roar of disapproval as I stood, open mouthed and wide eyed, for it seemed to me that he was being cruel to my Mum, just about squashing every breath out of her, lying on her side on the bed! Before I could say so though, they both roared at me to get out and stay out! I couldn't believe it. Mum shouting like Dad! I picked up my tiddler and retired, quaking in advance at the row I was going to get. Downstairs, I went into the garden and killed the little fish, swishing it down the lav. Strangely enough, nothing more was said about the affair, and it all blew over, or so I thought.

On the following Sunday, I stood watching my sisters getting ready for Sunday School, when father, in that dreadfully quiet voice that heralded the storm, told me to get my coat on.

"But I don't go to Sunday School," I quivered, wondering at my own daring in opposing him.

"Then it's high time you did, you bloody little heathen. You'll go, if I have to kick you up the backside all the way!" So saying, he flung me and my coat out of the door, muttering something about little snoopers. I snivelled all the way there, and Eva told me sharply to stop bawling, giving me a clip round the ear for good measure.

The Sunday School was large, cold and dark, being held in the huge basement hall underneath the Victoria Park Baptist church. There were about two hundred children gathered there, and they were singing lustily when I was ushered in by my sister. There was a tall thin man standing on a platform, a kindly looking soul with gold framed glasses and red cheeks. The classes were just groups of forms, three forms around a chair, where the teacher sat. I was placed in a class with girls of my own age, while all the boys sat on the opposite side of the hall. There were several men walking around to keep order, but it all looked quite interesting, and I felt that Sunday School might not be such a bad place after all. Besides, it would be easy to talk to God here and I might have some more prayers to be answered.

But my content was short lived. The girl beside me gave me a shove, so I promptly turned and trod hard on her foot. She was a nicely dressed, brown haired girl with big brown eyes, but there was no welcome for me in those eyes.

"I'll stand no nonsense from you," she whispered cuttingly, under cover of her hymn book. "That happens to be my father up there," nodding towards the platform, "and one word from me and you'll be punished."

"Alright, showoff," I shrugged. "And my father just happens to be head policeman of Bethnal Green, and one word from me and you'll go to prison." So we sat and bristled like two tom cats, and it was nearly nine years before we really spoke to each other.

My father was always the policeman when I was in trouble. When I got pushed off a swing, or some boys tormented me, I was always going to tell the head policeman, my father. This faith in the police is still widespread. I have a friend who, when widowed, asked a policeman neighbour if he would let her have an old police hat. This she keeps in prominent display on a hall table just inside the front door, and she is sure it deters unpleasant callers.

Unlike my imaginary father, this girl's father really was the Sunday School superintendent, and I envied her with all my heart. She really was a somebody, in that Sunday School.

Before we came out, we sang a closing verse, called a vesper. It was a nice quiet tune and I enjoyed it. Only one thing puzzled me though. The last line was 'Grace and peace and joy. Bisto.' Why on earth they had to put gravy powder on the end of that verse beat me. It was ages before I knew it was 'bestow'.

After a few weeks, I settled down and stayed the course, so that years later when my Dad complained about me being so damned holy, I smiled inwardly and longed to remind him that it was he who kicked me into the Kingdom of God, anyway. Yet he never went to church himself, only on the rare occasions of hatch match and despatch.

The Band of Hope was entirely different. Held on a Monday evening, it attracted so many children as to need two sittings. We would queue up for about three quarters of an hour, and the queue was so long by the time the doors opened, that there would be another three hundred or so waiting to get in when we came out. Some of the children came out and tagged on to the end of the queue again, so much did they enjoy it.

Yet it was a very simple meeting really. We sang cheerful hymns, flashed on a big screen, lovely hymns about drinking pure water and not yielding to temptation.

One favourite was

> Give me a draught from the crystal stream,
> When the burning sun is high

Not that any of us had even seen a crystal stream, but it was a nice gooey tune and we could really yell.

But the top favourite appealed to me very much, the words had so much meaning for me.

> As on the path of life we tread,
> We come to many a place,
> Where if not careful we may fall, And sink into disgrace.

There was a really rousing chorus which we yelled at the top of our voices.

> Don't step there, don't step there, don't step there,
> For if not careful you may fall, don't step there.

The drinker's path is one beset with many a hidden snare,

> The drinkers path is one beset with many a hidden snare,
> Oh, shun the drink shop's fatal spell, I warn you,
> Don't step there.

After the hymns, the lights were lowered and we had a story, illustrated by Magic Lantern slides. A deep hush settled over us as we listened to the lovely stories. Nearly always about poor children living in hovels, whose fathers drank away every penny. My Dad was a saint compared with these fathers. How we all wept, when father stole the blankets off the children's bed to take to the pawnshop for drink money. And we sobbed audibly when mother walked the streets in the snow to get help for her sick baby, clasped to her breast for warmth, while Dad lay in a drunken stupor on the bare boarded floor. Then, the minister or the vicar met up with the family, and when the dog collar went into the hovel, the sin went out. Father broke down and admitted the evil of his ways, all the family were saved, father got a job immediately; and they all lived happy ever after. This was the bit I found hard to swallow. I knew that even good men, when they lost their job, didn't easily get another. But I supposed the minister helped them, because the last picture showed them all well dressed and smiling, sitting in a well furnished room with flowers in a vase on the table, and even the sick baby had taken a miraculous turn for the better and was now a chubby darling sitting on father's knee.

Then the lights went up and we sang another hymn and made for the door, taking a ticket and signing the pledge, week after week. "I promise to abstain from all intoxicating drinks as beverages." I didn't understand the last bit, but this one thing I knew. That ticket was my all important pass to the Lycett Christmas party.

Every week, the signed ticket was handed in; they must have needed quite a staff to cope, and when the time came for the party, the party tickets were numbered according to the attendances made during the year.

The party was good fun, including a pantomime given by some of the children. One year I was chosen to take the part of one of the ugly sisters in 'Cinderella'. I wasn't very excited about this, because Eva kept teasing me and saying how well chosen I was for the part. "They must have taken one look at you and realised you wouldn't even need any make up," she laughed. But I did my best, knowing that I'd been chosen because I would speak up and be heard throughout the hall.

After the pantomime, a sing song, and then, the highlight of the party — the Present. We sat in rows, according to our ticket numbers, with the highest attendances in front. There, on display, was the most wonderful collection of toys. Dolls by the dozen, dressed in every hue, books and games and cars and wooden horses. We came out in turn, to choose one thing from the array. There was no time for sympathetic pondering though. Your mind had to be made up, before you got to the front. If you hesitated, you'd get handed anything the helper thought fit. A money box, or jig saw, maybe, or any ordinary thing.

Gwen and I, together with our cousin Jean, always contrived to get in the front row, with a full attendance record. We always wanted a doll, nothing else entered our heads and we'd even prepared our other dolls beforehand. "We are going to buy you a new sister," we'd say, as we set off.

We'd count the boys in front of us, knowing they could safely be relied on to choose something else, and then make our choice. "The doll in the pink dress, or if it's gone, the one in the blue. Then the blackhaired one... we had them all lined up in order of preference. Gwennie would always choose a blackhaired doll, probably because it was like her, with her tight black curls. That was apart from her one stringy strand in the front. She had a habit of sucking this curl, and it always hung damp and limp at the side of her face.

After the present we lost interest in the party, until the end, when we were given a big paper bag as we made our way out of the church. Into it went the inevitable orange, but what a store of other goodies beside! Nuts and sweets and chocolate, and a whole packet of figs! It was a Christmas feast in itself, and well worth the trotting those two miles there and back, rain or shine, every Monday evening.

But what if one of us couldn't make it? Maybe a bad cold or something would keep us away. Did we lose our front seat for full attendance? Not a bit of it! The one who made it, would hold out two hands at the doorway in the great push out, one hand to one helper and the other to another and like as not we'd get a pledge ticket thrust into either hand. No one noticed in that crush and we gleefully took home the extra ticket.

Four

There was always something going on in our street, you never saw it empty for long. The milkman came twice, even though the dairy was in our street. The first call was very early and he hung the cans of milk on the door-knockers. But he came back at midday, and this time he loitered, making half a dozen stops in the street. We took out our empty can, paid him for the morning half pint, and took a clean jug out for another penn'orth. He would dip his long handled metal measure into the churn of creamy milk and pour it into the jug, giving an extra dash as a bonus. He would stand and chat to the Mums and they'd call him a cheeky so and so. He'd stop and kick a ball for a few minutes with the boys, or pause to admire a new baby. At first, he just had a handcart, but after a while he had a horse, a good tempered beast who'd let us all give him a pat, or take a sugar lump from our hands. We all liked the milkman.

In the summer months, we loved the water cart. A slow, ponderous animal pulled this cart, and the water came out in a spray, the full width of the cart. He'd come down one side, turn in the court, and go back up the other, to be followed after about half an hour by a road sweeper. If it was very hot and the driver wasn't looking, we'd sometimes take off our shoes and socks and walk after the cart, letting the cold water spray onto our legs. Mum got mad at us if we did it, but if she was out shopping, we'd join in with the rest and it was good fun.

There was 'Ole moaney gabbert', too. Every morning we heard his coming down the street, calling out, "Ole moaney gabbert". He was the greengrocer, and it was years before I knew that his cry was meant to be "All morning gathered". Anyway, everyone called him 'Ole Moaney', but he was a very pleasant red faced man and his stuff was good. His prices were higher than Green Street or Roman Road, but then, you paid to have stuff brought to the door. Mum didn't get much from him, but, as she so often said, it paid to watch every penny. So she went, at least twice a week, either to Green Street or Roman Road. If you walked up Grove Road to the Aberdeen cross roads, there was a market in either direction. Roman was dearer than Green Street, but a little bit posher: not many second hand stalls or scruffy ones there, and not so many scruffy people either. So Mum mostly went to Roman, unless she wanted eels, because the best eel shop was in Green Street.

She always took two shopping bags, both made from real leather. They were chair seats which Dad had brought home from the upholsterers. She machined them, sewed on thick handles and cut a scalloped pattern all round the top. She'd buy the potatoes, four pound in each, because, like the sausages, you'd get one more this way. Four pounds for tuppence ha'penny was the usual price, although King Edwards were threepence.

The hearthstone man came twice a week, and sold both green hearthstone and whitening. We all knew that was the way to get a nice doorstep. First scrub it, then dip the green hearthstone in clean water and rub it on, then cover that with whitening. He did a good trade with us, because Mum whitened the copper and the lav floor as well as the front step. He was a thin faced little man, who always looked hungry. He was very polite and touched his cap when he gave us the change. I expect he was pretty poor, he needed to sell a lot of hearthstone to make much profit.

The shrimp and whelk man came on Saturday afternoon, soon after the pubs shut. Nearly everyone came out to buy shrimps or winkles for Sunday tea, and a pin was quite a usual accompaniment to the plate when we laid the Sunday tea table. First, you'd prise off the winkle's cap, stab it with the pin, and twirl it around and bring it forth in triumph from its shell. Then you'd dip it in vinegar, still on the pin, and pop it into your mouth. If the full ones and empty shells got mixed up on your plate, as they often did, then you'd have to blow into each one. They made a dull sound if full, and a whistling noise if the shell was empty.

The muffin man was a regular, too. He carried his tray of muffins on his head, covered with a white cloth, and rang a handbell as he walked. It always intrigued me that he never lost his balance, and that tray sat on his head as though glued there. It was winter when he came, and the sound of a little brass bell still makes me think of big fires and toasted muffins, all dripping with melted margarine.

How we loved Sunday tea! There was sometimes a jelly, or a head of celery, and in the summer a big cos lettuce. Mum would cut it in big chunks and you could fill the chunk with vinegar and crunch it. We never seem to meet with a real crunchy lettuce these days. Most weekends, Dad had his favourite delicacy: dutch herring. This we had to go and buy on a Sunday morning from the Jew shop in Green Street. We had to take a plate with us, and fight our way into the overcrowded little shop. Most people seemed to run out of things on Sunday morning, because it was always jam packed. Dad liked the bread there too, big shiny loaves covered with seeds on the scrumptious crust.

No one ever queued, so you just worked your way in towards the counter and kept on shouting, "A threeha'penny dutch herring please." At length the old Jew, in his greasy coat and cap, would grab the plate, roll up his sleeve and dive his arm into a vinegar filled barrel near the door, and come up with a slimy, slithery pickled herring, slap it on the plate and cover it with a scrap of plain paper.

One Sunday morning, Eva had been sent for the herring, a job we all hated; and when she reached home, the plate was empty! Fortunately, she found out before she knocked at the door, and she went skeltering back the way she had come. In the next street, she found Dad's herring lying on the pavement, too salty even to be eaten by a stray dog, though heaven knows how many might have sniffed it. Anyway, she picked it up, put it back on the plate and took it home without telling anyone. Poor Dad. So often things happened and we didn't tell. He did go so barmy if we told.

One day, our black cat pinched his Saturday steak from the frying pan. One minute, it was just beginning to sizzle gently, and the next, the pan was empty and the cat swearing under the sink. Mum dived after him with the copper stick and managed to retrieve the meat. She put it under the tap and back into the pan smartly, but knew she didn't have to say, "don't tell your father", to the onlooking girls. The cat might have gone into the canal in a sack if we told, as we well knew. So Dad ate his steak, germs and all, because, as Mum often said, "what eye don't see, 'heart don't grieve over."

Mum liked that cat, but she had her problems with him. Dad never allowed the cat on the bed, and one evening, going up in the semi darkness, Mum spotted him asleep on the bed. She grabbed a stinger, the small sharp cane she used on our legs, and whacked hard at the offender, only to find to her horror that it was not the cat on the bed, but Dad's best bowler. He never did find out what caused that dent line.

The cat was a dreadful thief, but he was a wonderful mouser and ratter. In fact, the feather factory welcomed him with open arms, and an open window too, and night after night he brought home a dead rat. We would hear his plaintive mewing outside in the yard and rush out to see what he had brought home. He never brought in his finds, but left them as offerings on the back doorstep. Occasionally it was not a rat, but a still wriggling shiny fish which he had caught from the canal. Once, it was a half cooked, still warm kipper! Not wanting trouble with the neighbours, Mum rushed and took it from him and threw it in the dustbin, but minutes later, old Tim was back with the kipper's mate, and this time he retreated behind the coal bunker to eat his meal in peace.

The only time he made a mistake was when he landed smack in the cold canal, while trying to catch a seagull. He came home a sadder and wiser cat, and Mum dried him and sat him by the fire.

He was not a jealous cat and was most protective towards my cat, a tiny ginger one, which we had trained to do lots of tricks. This cat played high jump with us, and would take his turn over the rope stretched across the garden. In fact, so used did he become to this jumping exercise, that he would run and leap over the rope if we left it there when perhaps we went in to tea, never thinking to run straight under. We made him a swing from a shopping basket hung on the clothes line, and this so delighted him, that he would climb in and sit and mew plaintively for a push whenever anyone passed by. At meal times, if father was not around, we would sit him up to the table, where he would eat daintily from a doll's saucer. I can't recall that he ever caught a mouse, but Tim was there to do that sort of thing.

Janet had a white cat, with one blue and one pink eye, a big fat lazy animal, who felt that his chief role in life was to keep himself clean. All our cats were 'doctored' toms, for Dad would tolerate neither 'shes' having kittens all over the place, or toms which had not been done, for they were stinking things, wetting up the walls and making the whole yard smell. No, our cats were nice clean healthy cats who caused no trouble.

We had a cats' meat man calling every day. He came along the street with a basket on his arm, calling "meeeeet, meeeeet" as he came. A veritable pied piper was he, with all the cats of the neighbourhood running at his heels. The pieces of meat were threaded neatly onto wooden skewers and he would throw down a skewerful to the customer's cats as he reached their doorway, collecting his penny on the way back. If the door was shut, he would leave the meat under the knockers and I often saw our Tim trying to balance on someone's door handle to reach a knocker full of meat. Today, we shove meat pieces on skewers, dress them up a bit and serve them in la-de-da restaurants, with fancy names like kebabs, but they always remind me of cats' meat.

When my husband was a small boy, he lived over a cats' meat shop. The horse flesh was delivered raw and cooked in the kitchen, so that the smell pervaded the whole house. As for the flies, half a dozen fly papers couldn't cope with them all. They were rowdy roughs, these cats' meat people, and had a bad name in the whole area. Sometimes on a Saturday night, they would fight amongst themselves, bringing out the big meat knives to threaten each other. The scared little chap upstairs would lie quaking in his bed, hoping that the lock would hold when the drunken meat men went chasing up and down the stairs.

We had other visitors to our street. There were several bakers, for the big combines were gradually beginning to vie with the little local men, and

Nevilles and Prices and the Co-op sent their big vans around. They would offer incentives to the women to try their bread, nicely wrapped in printed paper. Sometimes a whole week's bread would be free, and another time, there was a half tea service free if one used their bread for six weeks. Of course we did so, Mum was always on the look out for such offers, but as soon as possible, we reverted to the baker with the two wheeled handcart and the warm crusty loaves he carried. Some of the wrapped bread was steam baked, "bloody cotton wool", my father called it, and he wouldn't eat it, even for free.

The carbolic man called every week, pushing a little handcart and shouting his wares. Mum used a lot of carbolic, and would take out the smelly blue bottle to be filled with the whitish liquid every week. She used it in the lav, on the dustbin, down the drains, and in the water when she scrubbed, overlavish with it as with most things, and it was small wonder that her hands were always scarlet and cracked in winter. That was Melrose time. We all used Melrose. It was sold in a little square box and was a yellow, rounded, wax-like lump. We warmed it in front of the fire and rubbed it on our chaps. Not only Mum and Janet had chaps, although theirs were very bad, bleeding in the worst of the winter. We children always had chapped knees, for there were no tights or trews for us, or long trousers for our cousins. No, we all went out and got our knees wet and cold and got chaps and chilblains, and put up with it, accepting such discomfort as a normal part of winter life.

Chilblains were a common complaint every winter, especially on our feet. No fur lined boots for us. Mum firmly carried out Janet's old world remedy, old fashioned even by those standards, and today's children would die with horror. I wasn't a bit keen, and I'd keep quiet about my chilblains as long as I possibly could. But the itching eventually gave me away. I had to go and get the big 'jerry' from under the bed, squat down and produce as much water as I possibly could and then stick my itching feet in it while it was still warm! I can't see that it was a cure, for I seem to remember chilblains every year.

At one time, we had a tape man who called, with his pathetic little supply in an old pram. He was wizened and frail and ancient, and most horribly dirty. "Tape, tape," he would cry, stopping the pram every now and again to cough, a dreadful hacking cough. Mum took pity on him once, and bought a couple of yards of tape, so whenever he came along after that, he would stop optimistically at our door. Sometimes, Mum would buy linen buttons from him, which she used on workaday underwear. Pearl buttons would soon break in our big mangle, but the linen buttons would last and last. One day, the poor old tape man came along later than usual, and as luck would have it, Dad was already home from work, having finished an outdoor job early.

"Tape, tape," came the quavering voice, when I opened to his knock. "Not today, thankyou," I replied quickly, knowing that Mum was forbidden to buy at the door.

"Oh me dear, now ask your muvver, ask your muvver, do," appealed the old man, touching my elbow as he spoke. Poor tape man, he must have wondered what hit him. Dad rushed out of the door and knocked the old man's pram flying.

"Assault my daughter, would you," he yelled, unfastening his leather belt. The poor old chap grabbed his pram, took to his heels and ran, while Dad went in and let rip to Mum about encouraging beggars and tramps. We never saw the tape man again: he gave our street the go bye and I don't blame him.

There were a couple of tally men who came once, trying to get Mum to buy on the never never. Mum said No, quite firmly, but as she tried to close the door, one of the men put his foot inside, not knowing that Dad was standing there. With a terrific roar, he hurled himself at the man, a young Jewish looking individual. "I'll teach you to step uninvited into my house," he called, taking off his belt and lashing out. "An Englishman's home is his castle," he shouted, giving chase, and the neighbours all came to the doors to watch Joe Clark in his temper. The two men were quicker than Dad and were soon away, but I knew that Mum was in for a time of it after that. He always blamed her. "You encourage them," he would yell, "looking at them with your soft eyes."

He always felt bitter towards tramps and buskers and the like, but I suppose he had a point. One bitterly cold Sunday morning, just as we were finishing breakfast, a dirty old tramp called and asked if we would make him a drink of tea. "Just to warm me guts, Guv, he whimpered to my father who had opened the door. Dad must have had a very good night, because instead of the expected roar, he took the tramp's blue enamelled pot from him and filled it with hot sweet tea. The old fellow took it and shuffled away, muttering his thanks.

"Gone to sit in the park shelter, I expect," said Mum, half wishing she had dared give him bread as well. Five minutes later, Mrs Kay, from the corner house called. "Joe, did you give that old fellow some tea just now? He's just poured it down the drain and now he's knocking on another door." Dad didn't stop to change his shoes, but put on his cap and chased up the street. But the wiley old devil had seen the red light and was away on a tram before Dad could catch up and bash his brains in, as he had fervently vowed to do.

Occasionally, when there was a glut of anything, the barrow boys would come along, selling peas, or cherries, or ripe strawberries. Ridiculously cheap they were, even for those days, but there was no way to keep soft fruit and it was better to sell it cheap than to waste it all.

Today, modern man has really progressed. Gluts of fruit are ploughed into the ground, good food is chucked into the sea, God's bounty is thrown back in His face, to keep the prices up. We, who were poor folk, could sit on our doorsteps in the summer evening sunshine and eat a whole bag of cherries or Victoria plums, revelling in simple pleasures that today's kids never know.

The old rag and bone men who came round, were very popular. One pushed a hand cart and the other, obviously a more prosperous individual, had a little grey donkey to pull his cart. The hand cart man gave money, just a penny or two, for a bundle of rags, but the other, a rosy faced old chap, gave china. A little plate, for a couple of items, a cup and saucer for a fair bundle, and all three for a big load. How carefully they were chosen, these pieces of china! Possibly, you could match something this week with a piece from the previous week and the old man had all the time in the world. If we had rags, Mum would stand and ponder, trying to decide between a big thick cup for Dad, or a sturdy mug for one of us. She would talk over the decision with the rag man for all the world as though she was paying shillings for the items.

One day, when Rosie was playing with us in the street, the old man gave her a beautiful plate with roses on it. He had stopped and asked her what her name was, and when she smiled and told him "Rosie", he had patted her head and handed her the lovely plate for her very own, without asking anything for it.

The old iron man who came each week was a stingy old fellow. He would grope around in his pockets in the hope you might say, "It doesn't matter," but we knew him, and stood our ground until he handed over something for the leaking iron kettle or old fire irons we gave him. But we accepted the small coins gladly, because as Mum said, it was stuff we'd have thrown in the canal anyway, if he hadn't been coming round.

Sometimes, there were street singers, mostly poorly clad men or women, or even both together, who shuffled along in the middle of the road, singing in a croaky voice and looking optimistically up at the windows, or into the open doorways. Sometimes, people would throw down a penny, but often they went the whole length of the street without getting so much as a single coin. Poor things, they made me feel all lumpy in the throat, and if Eva wasn't around, I'd like as not have a good cry over them. Eva always called me a water cart, or a snivelling cry baby, if she caught me crying over nothing. But I wondered what they'd do, if they didn't get any money anywhere. Maudie's Mum said they only pretended to be poor, and that they went home to big houses on the train, or even owned motor cars, but I found it hard to believe, especially when they wandered up and down the street in the pouring rain, as they often did.

I remember one day when a lavender woman came. She sang in a high pitched voice, which was surprisingly clear, the old tune we all knew well.

> You buy it once, you buy it twice,
> It makes your clothes smell very nice,
> Scent your pocket handkerchief,
> Put it in your drawers,
> Sixteen full branches, one penny.

She carried her lavender in a big basket on her arm, and she had just reached our court when it started to rain, coming down suddenly and quite hard. The poor woman had no coat, so she folded her apron up over her arms and tried to shelter in the doorway opposite. It was a chilly day and within a few minutes the rain was an absolute downpour. Mum came to the door and stood looking across for a few minutes, and then called to the woman to come and shelter in our passage for a bit, so's she wouldn't get so wet.

"Aint you got a coat?" asked Mum, looking at the thin wet blouse. The woman shook her head and shrugged her thin shoulders. Mum stood for a few minutes, you could actually see her thinking. Then she went upstairs and came down carrying an old brown coat with a big fur collar. It was not a coat she wore, it was really very old, but was used as an extra blanket on our bed when the weather was very cold. I had often put it on, and played bears with the big fur collar when I was supposed to be asleep in bed.

Diffidently, she held it out and the woman's eyes lit up, and then actually filled with tears. "You're welcome," said Mum, "I never wear it."

Soon afterwards the rain stopped, and the woman went on her way dressed in the coat, handing me a bunch of her sweet lavender as she went.

"Don't tell your father," said Mum shortly, but I was so impressed by her kindness, that I saw no harm. "Mum gave the lavender woman the old brown coat off our bed, and the woman gave me all this lovely lavender," I told Dad excitedly when he came home that evening.

"I see," said Dad in his quiet voice, "I see." I knew immediately that I should have kept quiet, but it was too late. "Now I can clothe every old tramp and good for nothing devil that comes my way." His voice began to rise as the storm broke and I fled outside with my lavender, but not before I had seen Mum's tear filled eyes and the stricken look she gave me as he began his usual tirade.

The kids could perish with the cold, she'd be crying and whining for a new coat next winter, and blankets for the bed, but he'd swing first, before he put his hands in his pocket. He was always going to swing first, though I never knew then what he meant.

"Get up the stairs and give them my bloody best suit," he stormed. "Plenty more where that came from. I've only got to slave my guts out to dress you all, that's all."

He stormed out of the house as was usual when he was mad, and I knew that when he came home again he'd be drunk and would start all over again. If only I'd have thought before I spoke, I might have known what would happen.

"Big mouth," snarled Eva at me as I went upstairs, but Mum didn't say anything, she never did. Only went quiet and wore her sad face all evening.

Sometimes, we had an organ grinder to pay us a visit, and we would run up and crowd around him, joining in if he played the well known songs. He usually got more pennies than the singers, but the most lucrative buskers were a bunch of men who sometimes came with an organ. They were mostly young fellows, about six or seven of them, all dressed up as women. They wore high heeled shoes, loads of heavy make up with big cupid's bow lips, and big balloons down their fronts to make busts. The women, especially the rowdy ones, would join them and have a good laugh, shrieking as the dancing men showed their bloomers, all lace trimmed and hanging down over their knees, and maybe one of the women would go up to give them a penny and stick a hat pin in the huge bosom so that it exploded with a loud bang. What entertainment we enjoyed when they came. They did quite well for pennies, but earned every coin they got.

It was evening time when the tea chest men came. I could never work out why they came, or what they got out of it, but they would occasionally come half way down the street with a big horse and cart, laden with tea chests, each chest filled to the brim with broken bits of plywood. These they would give away, throwing them down in the roadway and calling to folk to come and get them. They were not much use for firewood, being hard to chop, but we children particularly gathered quite a store. The foil linings could be used for lots of things, and one summer we got two and a half chests at an angle, and there we had the most wonderful dolls' house. We lined it with wallpaper and spent weeks making cardboard and plywood furniture. When it was all finished, we put some of the mice in it and had great fun, watching them run over the chairs and tables we had made. Another time, we peopled it with caterpillars, but Mum drew the line when I tried catching black beetles from the hen run to put in. I was always in trouble for catching creepy crawlies, for I loved everything that moved, apart from worms. I still hate them, but my hatred probably stems from the day when two big boys in the park put a huge fat worm down my back. I can still remember how I screamed and screamed, until a passing man stopped and put his hand down my back and brought the pink wriggling thing up. I looked at it and was promptly sick.

The lamplighter was a nice man and we always ran to meet him, trotting with him from lamp to lamp as he lit the gas with a long pole which he carried over his shoulder. If it was winter, we would gather round the lighted corner lamp until our mothers called us in. Occasionally, we would persuade Gwen to climb up the lamp post and tie a rope from the crossbar at the top, so that we could swing around the post, heedless of the bruises we gave our shins in the process.

Of all the street callers though, our favourite was the gas man. Dear gas man, he went on being my favourite for many a year, yes, even after I was married.

He would kneel down in the passage, just by the door, and shake out the big pile of pennies from the meter onto the doormat. Then he'd stack them all up in piles of twelve, and count them into a cloth bag. But it was the next bit we enjoyed. He'd consult the meter, then the little book he carried, write out a receipt and hand it to Mum, with a little pile of pennies back again. The rebate, they called it, but how lovely it was. Mum would always give us one penny each. A whole penny in the middle of the week! Then she'd call over the fence to auntie Liz and ask her how much she'd got back. Then maybe, we'd have a cream doughnut or a cheesecake for tea, or even, if the rebate was good enough, a savaloy or faggot with pease pudding for supper.

This mouth watering delicacy had to be fetched in a basin from a faggot shop in Roman Road. It was a long way to walk, but it was smashing, especially with lashings of gravy. That's why we always took a big basin, so that they could give lots of gravy. We'd hurry home with the big hot basin full, and Mum would put it onto hot plates and we'd have it for supper. Never tastes the same nowadays if I make pease pudding and buy faggots, and as for a savaloy, I doubt whether a butcher would know what we meant. It was a big, hot, spicy red skinned sausage, and you just peeled off the skin and dipped it in the gravy and pudding. Lovely grub.

Some people had things like that for a dinner, but Mum always made it extra, making certain to cook us a good substantial meal every day. It's funny, thinking back, how well we ate. I think she'd have died with fright, had she lived to see the day when a joint of meat could cost a whole pound, or even more. We were well fed throughout our childhood and if we went short of anything, it was never good food.

The poor old 'tape man' always looked hungry.

Five

Victoria Park was our haven of delight. Even when we were quite young we were allowed to go there alone, and almost every morning of the school holidays, we set off, Gwen, Jean from next door, and me. Sometimes, Eva and the boys would accompany us, but mostly we went by ourselves.

With a ha'penny in our pocket, a couple of slices of bread and dripping and the everlasting doll apiece, we were gone for hours. We had two main roads to cross, but there was always a policeman on point duty at the 'Aberdeen' where there were buses to the City, and we never had any trouble crossing the road.

Not possessing a doll's pram didn't worry us in the least, we carried our dolls in a shopping bag and told them everything that was of passing interest.

When we reached the park gate, we would spend our ha'penny, usually on a big thick toffee bar which would last, if it was licked carefully and not chewed, until it was time to eat our bread and dripping. What dripping it was too! Usually beef dripping, liberally covered with the gravy which had jelled at the bottom of the basin. Mum would dig it out and cover the dripping, spread on thick crusty bread. Then a dash of salt and it was a sandwich fit for a king. Sometimes, it was pork dripping, smooth and creamy, with occasional bits of crackling stuck in it.

We sat on the grass, took the dolls out of the bag, and had a feast. Then we'd wash it down with a drink of water from the nearby fountain, where the old metal cups were chained to the edge, and drink only from the middle of the cup, not letting our lips touch the rim, as we had been taught. This way, we wouldn't get any germs.

There was a boating lake in the park, and we spent ages watching the boats. There were rowing boats for up to four people, but the men who rowed in the single boats skimmed along at a terrific pace. We would watch them round the little island in the centre of the lake, and try to see how many we could count before they came in view again. There was a chugging motor boat too, and it cost a penny to go right round the lake on that. We couldn't afford it, but we enjoyed watching other people have rides, and very occasionally we had one too. We'd line up, and hope that we'd get a side seat so that we could dangle our hands in the water, but it was all chance, and you couldn't hold back just to get a side seat. If you sat down the middle, that was that.

One of our favourite games was tormenting the parkie. He was not one of the ordinary park keepers, who patrolled the park dressed in a brown uniform with brass buttons. The parkie we tormented was in charge of the little island in the centre of the lake. This was approached by two bridges, one on either side, and a big notice stated that unaccompanied children under the age of fourteen were not allowed on the island.

We'd creep across the wooden bridge, knees knocking at our own daring, and sneak around the little winding paths with which the island was honeycombed. It was in truth a lovers paradise, for in every secluded spot was a seat, and right at the centre was a big red pagoda. Old men mostly sat there, warming themselves in the sunshine and yarning about the good old days. Some of them had birds, poor little finches or linnets in tiny cages tied up in a thick black cloth. We were too used to this spectacle to think of it as cruel, but the poor little birds, deprived of light and freedom, would sing their very heart out as the warm sun shone on the black cloth of their prison. The old men would discuss the merits of their birds, whom they loved in their own way, and never think of themselves as heartless. I think that some of today's tough youngsters would have mugged these old men, not to steal their pitifully few pennies, but to set free the little birds. But we saw no wrong in it; lots of people had linnets and finches.

Anyway, we'd tiptoe around until we came upon him, the king of the little kingdom, in his plain grey suit and trilby hat.

"Parkie", we'd yell, taking to our heels. But we'd split up and race off the island in two different directions, using both bridges to make our quick getaway. Poor man! He who hesitates is lost, but he never seemed to learn this, and while he was deciding whom he had best chance of catching, we were off the island and meeting up with each other by the bird aviary, which stood about equidistant from both bridges.

There was a white and green cockatoo in this aviary, supposed to be a wonderful talker. It could swear too, but I never heard it say anything other than "Pretty Polly".

Further round the park was another aviary where there were pheasants and Indian geese, and hard by, a rocky enclosure with a few goats. These last were great fun, because they would eat anything we pushed through the bars, and the boys fed them old paper bags and bus tickets as well as the grass.

There were several lots of swings, each in a well fenced enclosure and presided over by a 'swing lady'. She had a little hut inside the shelter each lot of swings possessed, where she could brew tea, or bandage knees, or chat with her friends, while keeping a watchful eye on the children. She was most vigilant and woe betide any rough who tried to push a small girl off a swing, or who dared to cheek her.

Swing ladies must have been chosen for their toughness, their word was law and no one ever got the better of them. They wore navy hats like the school Nitty Norah, and were equally to be feared. I've seen a swing lady turn everyone out and lock the gates when she saw any misbehaviour. No one ever stood up on her swings and vandalism was a word we'd never heard. Oh, we weren't a saintly lot, far from it, but we were so much more easily satisfied in those days.

But they were very fair women in their dealings with us, and on a busy day, they'd line us up and time our swinging so that everyone got a turn. There was a big rounder too, a number of thick ropes hanging from a central pivot. Each rope was looped with a metal end. We stuck our elbow through the loop and tucked it under our armpit, gripped the rope and hung on for grim death, running faster and faster round the post until the rope swung out and our feet left the ground. Some of the bigger girls could get their bodies almost horizontal. But I was a bit scared of that thing and having seen several broken limbs there, I preferred the comparative safety of the swings.

They had a sand pit there but it was a bit grubby, and surrounded by a climbing wall of concrete made to look like a castle, it was always crowded with boys. So there was not much point in playing there, trying to pretend it was the seaside.

One morning I was sitting in the shelter waiting for Gwen to finish swinging, when a woman with two babies in a pram came up and started talking to me. I could never resist babies, and although these were not of the particularly clean variety, I was soon pushing the squeaky pram up and down the shelter.

After a little while, the woman, a skinny poorly clad person with filthy fingernails, asked me to mind the babies while she went to a shop nearby. "Just outside the gate," she said, "I shan't be a few minutes." I nodded, but pointed out politely that I didn't think there were any shops near the gate.

"Oh, just a little way along," smiled the woman. "I'll bring you back a bar of chocolate if you'll look after them."

For a while, I went on pushing the pram, but it was a chilly morning and I was soon anxiously looking for the return of the babies' mother. Gwennie had finished swinging and was getting fidgety.

"Let's go," she kept saying, but I shook my head. "I can't leave these poor babies alone. I'm in charge."

After a time, both babies began to cry, they were getting as fed up as I was. I didn't fancy nursing them, the little one smelt a bit and the bigger one at the bottom end of the pram was more than merely smelly.

So I just sat, and sat, and as the morning wore on, Gwen began to grizzle too. She was hungry also; I was in charge of her as well as these rotten babies, and if I didn't soon take her home, she'd run off by herself and go home alone, and then I'd be in trouble. This was too much for me and eventually I burst into tears myself. There we were, all howling together, and at last the swing lady realised that something was wrong.

"What's the trouble?" she asked, in her thin sharp voice. "Why don't you get along home and take these kids with you?"

I looked at them through my tears. I didn't really think Mum would like them, and besides, I didn't want to go to prison for stealing them.

"They aren't mine," I blubbered, and out came the whole story.

"But you've been here about four hours," she exclaimed. "That woman isn't coming back, you mark my words." She sent a boy to find a park keeper, and he in turn fetched a policeman. At the sight of his uniformed figure, my tears fell the faster; and when he opened his notebook and asked where I lived, I nearly had hysterics. At last, he took the pram with its squalling occupants and wheeled them away.

"Oh, please, don't take them to prison," I sobbed, "they haven't done anything wrong."

"That's alright ducks," said the swing lady, "they'll go to a nice place where they'll clean them up and give them a good feed." I'd never seen her with so kindly a face before, and I dried my eyes.

"What about their Mum, she'll be so cross with me," I said fearfully, but the swing lady shook her head. "She won't be back," she sniffed, "and if she does come, I'll give her a piece of my mind."

At the gate, I hesitated. I hadn't got much out of this morning's work. "If she comes, and brings me the bar of chocolate she promised, will you tell her I did look after her babies all the morning, and maybe she'll give you the chocolate to mind for me." The swing lady nodded and we ran all the way home, to where our anxious Mum was waiting at the corner of the court.

"That'll teach you not to talk to every bloomin' baby you meet," said she, but she wasn't really angry, only worried in case we were not home before Dad got in.

Most of our trips were far less eventful though, and we wandered at will through the big park, where we had names for all the lanes and footpaths. There were peacocks there, and we would stand for ages waiting for them to open their tails, and a herd of deer who came up and pushed soft noses into our hands. There was a big glasshouse and we would walk quietly through, looking at all the wonderful flowers there, and sniff the hot humid air.

Something has gone wrong with our modern world. I could never imagine my grandchildren being allowed out for hours and hours alone like that. They'd most likely be assaulted, or worse. Yet in all those years, we only once met with trouble, and that we thought was extremely funny.

We had been sitting playing with our dolls on the grass, and a man was standing nearby, watching us thoughtfully. We didn't take much notice and there was no one else around, just us, and the big expanse of grass.

Suddenly, he came nearer, much nearer, exposing himself as he did so. We jumped up, packing the dolls quickly into the bag, eyeing him warily. He had a queer look on his face, and somehow, I didn't like it. I tried hard not to look in his direction, but Gwen and Jean started to laugh, commenting on the size of what they saw, comparing it with our cousins. "Ain't it a whopper," they shrieked, yelling with glee.

I joined in then, but tried to usher them away. "I think its going to rain," I said firmly. The man just stood there hesitatingly, a glazed expression on his face, then he turned his back on us and wandered away without a backward glance. Our childish laughter was probably the best answer to the situation.

In spite of my warning not to tell Dad, Gwen could hardly wait to get into the house before she came out with it, and Dad fumed and carried on and said we were not to go to the park again. But after a week or so, it was all forgotten, though Mum always warned us to run and tell the nearest park keeper if we saw anything like it again.

One day, a kindly looking man gave us a bag of pears, but as soon as he had gone, I threw them in the waste bin, telling the others that they were probably poisoned. We always threw away any sweets given us by strangers, thinking in our innocence that it was the sweets themselves that were harmful and the reason why we were always warned not to accept anything from strangers.

There was one particular avenue of trees, known to all as 'the Prom'. On Sunday mornings, all the courting couples walked up and down and all the sets of young people from the nearby churches, dressed in their Sunday best. It was a real guide to the who's who of the day, and we knew who was going out with whom. When we got a bit older, we would watch to see who was walking with Eva, and if it was the same young man more than twice running, we knew something was going on. Yes, the Prom was the place to show off your new clothes and smart hats and I longed to be old enough to walk up and down with a young man.

Not far away was a little group of trees, with seats around in a circle, and here a mission group would meet every Sunday morning. They had a small harmonium, and a big blue banner proclaiming 'The Out and Out Mission'. They were a devout group of about fifteen people, and they sang rousing hymns with jolly choruses. We would go and sit on the seats and listen, and I'd hope for my favourite.

Look and live, my brother live, look to Jesus now and live.
'Tis recorded in His word, Hallelujah, that you only have to look and live.

I used to sit and wonder where I had to look. I gazed at their shining faces, especially at one badly crippled young fellow whose face absolutely beamed, and thought how happy they looked. People might snigger as they walked past, but they seemed to have something special. They called each other brother and sister just like the Salvation Army, but they didn't have a band, only this little thing where one of them sat and pedalled away like mad.

Years later, I met the people who ran this mission and found out that the badly crippled fellow was the only son of the family. He didn't have much to look so happy about either, because he suffered terrible pain from his crippled legs and he couldn't get work either. When there wasn't nearly enough work for the fit, then the weak and helpless had to make do as best they could. There was no Welfare State to care, so he didn't really have much to sing about.

Only once can I recall the park being shut for several weeks. This was at the time of the General Strike in 1926. I didn't understand all the whys and wherefores of it, I only knew that there were soldiers camped out in big bell tents in the park and the gates were shut, apart from a small one where a sentry stood guard. We would walk along Grove Road where it ran between two sections of the park, and talk to the soldiers through the bars. I suppose it was alright to talk to strange men when iron spikes separated us. Steve and Will were particularly keen on doing this, and the soldiers would tell them of the foreign countries where they had been stationed. It all sounded very exciting, and I think that Will made up his mind from then on that the Army was the life for him.

Everyone kept saying that the strike was terrible, and my poor aunties set out to walk all the way from Bethnal Green to Knightsbridge every day, since there was no transport. One morning our little dog Peggy followed them, and when they got as far as Aldgate, they managed to get a lift on a lorry. Peggy had disappeared in the crowd, and when they came home at night, they were very upset to think that she was lost.

Although Dad was very tired, having walked to work and back, he got out the dog's lead and walked all the way to Aldgate in the hope of finding her. He had no luck, but about a week later she came scratching at the door; thin, muddy and starving, but delighted to be back with her family once more.

On summer evenings, the band would play in the park at weekends, and although it cost twopence to go and sit in the enclosure, you could hear all you wanted from the grass outside. Very occasionally we went there with Mum and Dad for a stroll, instead of going to bed at our usual time of half past seven. We would listen to the band and Dad would tell us all the names of the trees and flowers, and the history behind the big memorial fountain, and we would really enjoy his company.

On the way home, we'd call at the Crown pub, just outside the park gates, but Dad had a poor opinion of people who left kids outside pubs all evening, so he would only stop for one drink, bringing us out a big arrowroot biscuit to munch while he and Mum had their drink.

He wore his best suit on these occasions, with a gold chain across his waistcoat, and his bowler hat and best boots. My Dad looked a real toff when he went out. He was always fussy about dress though, and never went to work as many men did, with just a scarf around their neck and no collar or tie.

Every morning he held out his hand for a clean white folded hankie, which Mum gave him together with his dinner shilling and two small packets of sandwiches. The sandwiches always had to be in two packs, so that he could slip one into each coat pocket without showing a big bulge. He would never dream of going to the drawer and getting a hankie for himself, it was part of the ritual to have it handed to him.

Once, when Mum had flu and I had to get up and make the sandwiches, I omitted this and he stood with his hand held out. "Don't I get a bloody hankie?" he asked, in an injured tone.

Sometimes, we would all go out for an evening trip and take a bus to the City and walk all the way up to Oxford Street. Oh, the excitement of looking in the shop windows and seeing the things posh people wore and used. Dad would stand and gaze at the furniture shops, showing Mum the merits of the various things, pointing out what was good and what was just shoddy veneer. I was terribly proud of Dad, and felt that he knew nearly everything about everything.

Six

On the end of Dad's watch chain was a small gold locket, and inside was a photo of Rosie, my dear little sister, after whose tragic death my mother began to look older, and stopped singing as she worked. Indeed, for ages she never even laughed.

I was four and a half when Rosie was born, and remember creeping into the bedroom to see my new little sister. At least I was glad she was another girl. I was allowed to push the pram up and down the court, though not old enough to take her out on my own. But when Eva was with us, we would all go to the park together. Rosie had golden curls, a complete contrast to Gwen, with her tightly curled black locks. Her cheeks matched her name and she was altogether an adorable child.

When she was four, she fell sick one day, and that evening Dad took her to the doctor. A very rare occasion in our home, but Dad said he was worried and didn't like the look of her. She wasn't very ill, just sick and pale and headachy, but towards evening she became much more lively and began to look better. She had a fork in her little hand and was helping to spear pickled onions from a jar, laughing with glee whenever she caught one.

Early next morning, we awakened conscious of unusual noise. A strange voice on the stairs and a sound of sobbing. I crept out onto the landing and saw my Mum, her old brown overall tightly wound round over her nightie, her eyes red with weeping. One of the aunties took me by the hand and she too was crying.

"Go back to bed Dods, there's a good girl. Rosie is very ill."

We all three sat up in bed and listened. Now we heard the unbelievable, a man crying, deep shaking sobs that frightened us all. As Mum passed by our door, we called out and she put her head in the room, her white face with its red weepy eyes a never to be forgotten sight.

"Get up now," she said quietly. "Rosie is dead and there's nothing anyone can do."

Dead! It just wasn't possible. Not our baby. Other people's babies died, but not ours.

We got up and made ready for school. No one queried our lack of breakfast and we went out into the quiet street. When we reached the Infants Department, I hesitated with my hand on the knob, then shrank back. If I went in, then I might start crying and Eva was always teasing me for this. Yet Rosie had recently started school and I always took her in and helped her with her coat.

I ran up the stairs and sat down at my desk. After a time, the Headmistress of the Infants came in and stood talking to the teacher. They both looked in my direction and then called me out.

"Your little sister isn't at school today," said the Head kindly.

"No, she won't be coming any more. She's dead." I tried hard to speak as though it was of no consequence, looking straight ahead and concentrating on the window pane and a sparrow outside.

"Oh, my God!" The Head turned away abruptly and I went and sat down again, without a tear. Somehow I mustn't cry.

I sat there and wondered what Rosie was doing. Was she really there, above the bright blue sky, as we sang in Sunday school? Had they given her a white gown and a golden crown? I couldn't really see why God had to have her. There were so many other children He could have picked on. But then I suppose He was entitled to take the best, just as my Dad was the only one allowed to pick any flower he wanted from our garden.

The next days were nightmarish. We were there and yet not there. We were fed and washed and put to bed, but it all had an unreal quality. Mum didn't come in to kiss us goodnight, the aunties did it instead, and Dad talked in a hoarse kind of whisper and didn't shout once.

We all went up to Green Street to buy new clothes. Black coats and dresses and little black felt hats like pudding basins. Trimmed with black ribbons for Eva and me, and Gwen's white trimmed because she was the youngest. Our new dresses were black and white check and Mum bought yards of black velvet for our Sunday dresses. Black bordered hankies and black scarves; and Mum of course had black jet beads.

She took us in the front room, where Rosie lay on the big round table, covered with a white blanket. Not that any blanket could warm that little marble figure. She was dressed in a white nightie, with thick lace at the sleeves and neck. Never had I seen anything so beautiful as that little statue, in its white lace shroud, surrounded by the golden curls.

"Perhaps she isn't really dead," I whispered, but Mum burst into tears and I wished I had not said anything.

Then they came and took her away, and I listened while they talked about post mortems and such like; and how the doctor was exonerated from blame. He couldn't have known that night that it was meningitis, and by next morning, when Dad ran for him, it was too late. He must have been a very young doctor at the time, and it was probably his first death, because it was he who had sat crying at Rosie's bedside.

Now, forty five years later, he is still in the same practice, one of the grand old men of Bethnal Green.

Now the talk of hearse and horses took on a new meaning, for it was real; and this was one funeral when we wouldn't laughingly get the bucket ready at the door to beat old Mrs Kay to it. There was the usual collection among the neighbours and they all gave liberally. Then they gave a huge wreath, the 'Gates of Heaven'. That was what they always gave, if enough money was collected. Golden metal gates stretched across pillars of flowers, with a white dove at the base. 'From the Neighbours' it said, in big purple letters. The wreaths were lined up in the street outside the front door for all the neighbours to see and they all came along and stood in silence. Then they began to gather, crowding either side of our door, as we always did ourselves at other funerals and I peeped through the upstairs window to see the horses arrive.

But just when they were due, auntie Maisie put on our new black hats and coats and took us out, much to my disappointment. Only Eva was allowed to go to the funeral. Auntie took us for a bus ride to a distant park, but there was little enjoyment in it. She herself was upset, and we were fed up at missing all the excitement. I'd much rather have been sitting in that big, horse drawn coach than riding on a bus.

By the time we got home again, they were all back at the house and the tightly drawn blinds, shut all through the street, were open again; and the aunts and uncles were eating plates of ham and tongue, all seated around that big round table where the little body had lain. Disconsolately, we wandered out into the back garden and began sorting out Rosie's toy box, sharing her little treasures among us, and even fighting a bit over who should have what. Talk about the scripture, 'They parted my raiment among them,' I have often thought when I've read the Easter story, of us quarrelling over those little possessions.

This funeral was not like most of the street funerals I knew. There was no beer, it didn't turn into a sing song or a pub crawl as so often happened, and before long, they all left, leaving us alone with our grief.

That death had a profound effect upon us all, and changed our life in some ways. There was no radio, no gramophone even, in our house, and nothing broke the quiet stillness of those weeks that followed. Dad sat in his seat, watching the pigeons, and Mum sat with folded hands, not even knitting, just doing nothing, a thing I'd never seen before.

Our slightest headaches were cause for coddling and fussing and a mild bilious attack saw us being rushed to the doctor.

The aunties did their best to help us over the bad patch, and they started taking us out with them quite a bit, so it was only now that I really made the acquaintance of my great aunt Rose. She was Janet's younger sister, who lived in Hackney. Normally, she didn't bother with us very much, she was far more fond of our cousin Jean who visited her regularly, but we had been occasionally to visit our great grandmother Piper, aunt's mother, who lived with her.

Great grandmother Piper was a domineering old lady in her nineties, and when we visited she would bring out her Ludo board and demand that we sat and played with her. She always insisted on being red, and the red corner of the board was absolutely worn away, where Grandma Piper got excited and her thumb kept trembling on the edge of the board.

One day I caught her cheating, flicking the dice over to a six. I had been suspicious of this for some time, and when I caught her red handed, I jumped up and yelled that I didn't play with cheats. Aunt took me by the shoulders firmly and sat me down again.

"Get on with the game," she commanded firmly. "When you are ninety, you can cheat too."

I sat down again, but made faces at her behind her back, which got me a smart rap on the knuckles from the old lady. I wasn't very keen on her, anyway, she was almost too old to be real. Her skin was thin, almost like tissue paper and it worried me lest she got it torn. Once this happened, she might split all down, and come tumbling out of it and bleed all over. It was a nightmarish thought and I wasn't very happy being left alone with her. She wore black beaded blouses and long black skirts, a black shawl pinned with an enormous diamond brooch, and her snow white hair was piled in a neat little bundle on top of her head. Her skin showed through, all pink and soft looking, but that was the only soft thing about her. With piercing, deep sunk eyes and a very long nose, she was altogether forbidding in appearance.

German born, she had been travelling with her family to Australia and they had stopped ashore in England. Janet said they had been shipwrecked, but I never found out whether this was so. Anyway, while they were in England the little Rosalie had been taken ill, and was so sick that the family went on to Australia leaving her with relations. It was intended that she follow at some later date, but maybe travel for a child alone was pretty impossible in those days; at any rate, she never joined her own family, and when I knew her she was the matriarchal head of a big family of her own.

Her sons were all business men and owned some thriving concerns between them; her youngest daughter Rose married a German, and married well, and only little Janet and her other sister Eva who lived in our court, didn't do well in life. They were the poor relations, and as far as our wealthy

Piper relations were concerned, they could stay poor.

Privately, we always referred to aunt Rose as 'yer Aunt' and even Mum, who liked us to be polite, joined us in this nickname. This was because her husband Harry, always referred to her as 'yer Aunt,' when talking to Mum.

These were our posh relations. Their house was a big one of the type which has now sadly degenerated into flatlets and overcrowded dwellings, but in those days Hackney was something, and a cut above Bethnal Green. The hall of the houe was a wide high one, and when I entered it, I would gaze in awe at the chairs and table it contained and compare it with our narrow passage where there was barely room to pass.

My aunt had a maid too, though she always called her 'the girl'. My Mum referred to her as 'yer Aunt's poor Skivvy' and she certainly had to toil and toil in that house. Aunt would sit and read and cook and tidy up, but Skivvy was always on the go, rubbing and scrubbing. When Skivvy, who was a poor, thin angular woman, finally left, her aunt made do with a daily, and by the time I was visiting her frequently, she made do with a char for a few mornings weekly.

But she had other signs of wealth, to my mind. She had carpets on all her floor and the stairs, a shiny piano in the big parlour, a gramophone with lots of records, and she possessed the very first wireless I had ever heard. How it fascinated me to put on the little black earphones and listen to someone really talking, miles away! If Gwen and I were both there together, we would sit in silent ecstasy with one earphone each, listening to whatever programme was on.

Hardly anyone in our school had a wireless then, and I would boast to my friends about it. Later on, she was the first person I ever knew to have a loudspeaker installed, and even now, the football results given out over the air take my mind back to those far off days when we sat like little mice while uncle tutted or oh-d about the results.

Uncle Harry adored his wife. Like Janet, she was extremely small, but she was much more sharp featured than my beloved Grandma, and her hair was a dull mousy brown. She had a large firm bosom, but when I leaned my head on her one day, I was surprised to find it hard and bony. I mentioned this to Gwen, who nodded wisely. "I think she sticks teacups inside her stays," she said. Whatever the truth, she was well whaleboned all down, though all the stays in the world couldn't stop her looking like a little teddy bear in her brown fur coat.

When uncle came home from his office, he would bend over his wife, kissing her fondly and with a lingering that I found surprising. "And how has my darling been today?" he would ask. Then he'd put on his slippers and light his smelly old pipe, ignoring whichever of his great nieces who happened to be there, and talk of how he had saved old so and so a couple of hundred pounds. I never knew exactly what he did for a living then, but he must have been an accountant, from the way all his talk was about books and money.

He owned quite a few houses in Bethnal Green, and a big bungalow near Southend, but according to my father he was a tightfisted landlord who squeezed every penny out of his tenants and did nothing for them.

When Mum was a girl, he and his brothers had owned a large boot and shoe factory, and it was in this factory that Mum had first worked. Poor little Bertha! She often told me about the first week she went there. Uncle had walked through the factory and looked at her feet. "Can't have you working for me in those shabby old boots," he told her. "Get yourself measured for a decent pair at once." So Mum went home in brand new boots, thrilled to bits at her uncle's bounty. That was, until pay day came and she found he was stopping her sixpence a week from her three and six, until the boots were paid for.

Dad didn't like the old man one bit. They had had terrific arguments in the past, of which I was too young to get the gist, but they were all about the new National Insurance scheme. Uncle thought he had found a way round paying the employer's share and my hot-headed father had called him a twisting old bugger to his face and forbidden Mum to visit there.

They had big parties there occasionally, when the aunts let their hair down and joined in singing all the latest songs. Lottie used to sing a pathetic solo about a poor blind boy, and they all joined in a riotous chorus which went:

'Don't send my boy to prison, it's the first crime what he's done.' The men played jokes on each other, the prize one being a pouring of piccalilli down each other's trousers. All these excitements came to us as hearsay however, for as I said, we were not on visiting terms. But after Rosie died, yer aunt started having us to Hackney for the day on Saturdays, taking turns with Jean.

I always enjoyed my trip there, and looked forward to my turn. For one thing, she always left me to my own devices during the morning, when she was busy with the dinner, and I could read whatever I wanted to. She never said I shouldn't read the *Red Letter,* or *East Lynne,* or even the daily paper: as long as I was quiet I could please myself. I would creep up to the big parlour and pick out *God Save the King* or *Good King Wenceslas* with one finger on the shiny piano, singing to myself as I played.

It was thrilling to go shopping with yer aunt, and the biggest thrill of all was to go to Woolworths. I used to stand inside the door and take a deep breath. 'Nothing over Sixpence' it proclaimed in big gold letters, and I used to imagine what I would do, if only I had a sixpence. Why, I could buy anything in the whole shop! Saving a sixpence was from then on, my great ambition.

Once, aunt Rose bought me a row of beads. She let me choose, but vetoed my choice because it was green.

"I wouldn't let you bring them in the house," she said, "if you had the green ones. It's terribly unlucky to have anything green."

On one occasion, I had walked all the way to Hackney when it was my turn, dressed in my new coat. A lovely green one it was, with a grey fur collar. When I reached the house, she opened the door and held up her hands in horror. "Oh, Dol, fancy coming here in a green coat!" she exclaimed, "Your Mum should have known better. Can't understand her getting you a green coat in the first place." My face fell, and the lovely coat assumed sinister proportions. "It was cheap aunt, she got it in a sale. It was only twelve and six."

"Not surprised," snorted my aunt. "You'll break a leg, or get run over in that coat, you mark my words." All this time, I stood hopefully on her doorstep praying that she wouldn't send me packing to walk the two miles home again.

"Tell you what," she said at last, "take the coat off and roll it up and put it in the shed. Go the back way, so's you don't bring it through the house. You'll have to stay home if it isn't warm enough to go out without a coat this afternoon though, because I'm not walking out with you in that thing."

There were lots of other things that were unlucky too, as well as green. It was unlucky to sit on a table, to turn a thing right side out if you'd put it on inside out in the morning, to pick up a dropped glove (you didn't lose it, you merely got someone else to pick it up for you). If you went out and remembered something you'd left at home and went back for it, you had to sit down and count ten before setting out again. To open an umbrella indoors was unforgivable and to break a mirror was the absolute end, for then there was no way of avoiding seven years of bad luck! All these things, and many more like them, were aunt's religion, and she never tired of telling me how true she had found them to be.

Besides taking me to Woolworths, she sometimes took me to the pictures, and what a thrill that was. I had only been with the penny rush before that. The penny rush was held on a Saturday afternoon in a cinema just off Roman Road, and it was just what its name implied. My cousins made it a regular Saturday treat, and Eva often went with them, but none of them liked taking me. As we hurried along, clutching our orange or bag of peanuts, they would talk between them of Norma and Richard Talmadge and lots of other stars, but all I did was to pray like mad that no one would kill anyone or fire any guns.

When the doors opened we all rushed in, and for some reason that I could never fathom at the time, they all made for seats near the back and only the late comers sat in the front rows. As soon as the film started, the piano would start to play, the pianist dressed in a long black skirt with a white fancy thing on her head a bit like a Lyons nippy.

As soon as things got going, the piano would play loud banging music and I'd grip my hands on the seat and shut my eyes tight. Just in case anyone fell down dead. When a car came towards me on the screen, I was dead scared in case it came right out and ran me over, and when the cowboys and horses galloped in my direction, I would shoot under the seat and stay there.

If however the picture was sad, I would burst into tears and have to be taken outside in disgrace for making a noise. Mum and Dad once took us to see Charlie Chaplin in 'The Gold Rush' as a very special treat, but I broke my heart over the poor little man having to stew his boots for food.

"Oh, please, please," I cried aloud, "please can't anyone give him some food?" So, all in all, no one was very keen on taking me to the pictures. But when I grew a bit older and learnt to control my emotions, nothing delighted me more than being taken to the pictures by aunt Rose. Even the cinema she frequented was different, it didn't smell of smoke and oranges and sweat; there was a smartly dressed young lady who walked around spraying something into the air, and it smelt more like the perfume department of a big store.

The pictures we saw were nicer too: we never saw cowboys and indians there, but there were ladies and gentlemen kissing each other and holding hands and getting married and riding in lovely carriages. Or else they were dying gently in big beautiful beds, even better than aunt Kate's. "Kiss me Charles, and be good to baby," would flash on the screen, and the audience in aunt's type of cinema would read quietly, and just sob gently, if it was very sad. I would keep putting out my tongue to catch the tears as they rolled down my cheek, lest aunt should see me crying and not take me again. The piano played soft haunting music that made you want to keep on swallowing hard, and when you eventually came out into the bright sunshine, you could pretend you had something in your eye and keep on wiping it.

But aunt had developed a sudden cold too, and had to keep on sniffing, so we'd sniff and wipe our way home, where the two dogs would give us a boistrous welcome and aunt would make tea, talking all the time about what she'd have done, had she been the heroine. "She was too soft with him, don't you think, Dol," she would call from the kitchen and, thrilled to be talked to as an equal, I would discuss with her the merits of the film.

At the penny rush, everyone read the captions out loud.

"Oh leave me sir," we would all call out, as the maiden struggled with the villain. Oh, we had incentives to become fast readers in those days. Perhaps today's children would become better readers if the T.V. went back to the old silent days for its stories and children had to use their brain to read, instead of being spoon fed with all their entertainment.

It was not until the era of the 'talkie' that people like aunt Kate and Janet went to the pictures and I'll never forget when Mum and auntie Liz persuaded aunt Kate to go to see her very first film, 'The Singing Fool'.

Everyone was singing 'Climb upon my knee, Sonny boy,' and aunt Kate set off in joyful expectancy. What a scene they had with her when she came home! She cried and cried all night, and half the next day too, standing at the corner and wiping her eyes on her apron, the tears making rivulets down her powdered face.

"Oh my Gawd, it was lovely. I haven't slept all night for thinking about it."

'When aunt Kate went to the pictures' became a talking point all through the family for weeks after that.

I had another reason for longing to go to aunts, too. Her younger son Herman, owned a typewriter, the very first one I had ever seen, let alone touched. And he, dear Bert, would put a sheet of paper in it and let me sit and type. I was almost speechless in his presence because he had written a book and had it published, and though no one would let me read it, I knew how clever he must be. I read through lots of his other books though, and he never dreamed of saying I wasn't old enough.

What affluence there was at this house! They even owned their very own deckchairs. (The only time I'd sat in a deckchair was when someone in the park had got up and handed us their tickets because the three hours were not up that they got for their twopence.) When the sun shone, I could sit on the lawn in a deckchair and read grown up books and pretend that I was very rich. There was a cherry tree and when the fruit was ripe, Bert would come out and pick a few cherries to share with me.

Next door, was a Salvation Army Mother and Baby Home. If I climbed the wall, I could look down into the cots and prams out in the sunshine, with lovely little babies lying in them. Aunt used to tut and say they were all very sad and the mothers no better than they should be, but I thought the babies were lovely and said so.

One sad day, aunt was taken suddenly ill and rushed to hospital for an operation. Uncle came to tell us when it was over. "A lion," he said, "a lion, yer aunt is." He had been drinking to celebrate the news that his darling was going to pull through. His hat, perched on his head at a rakish angle, tilted forward over his eyes every time he leaned his head against the wall. "A brave little lion," he repeated, pushing the hat back again. "A brave little lion." He ambled off up the street, still muttering, and Janet ran along to tell the good news to her sister Eva.

"Well," said our Eva, when he had gone, "so now we'll all be off visiting the lion of Judah." We giggled at this, because we sung about the lion of Judah in Sunday School.

For the Lion of Judah shall break every chain
And give us the victory again and again.

Privately, the nickname stuck, and my sister always referred to yer aunt as the lion of Judah.

Seven

Eva had just started work about this time, and had entered the grown up world where we could not hope to follow. She was allowed to stay up long after we went to bed, and sometimes Mum and Dad went to the pictures, telling Eva to send us to bed at eight o'clock. On these occasions, she had her friend in, and we would sit on the top stair and listen to all their talk when we were supposed to be asleep.

She now had her own money to spend as she liked, and was even allowed on the little island in the park. Lucky thing. She saved up carefully for her clothes, for she had a wonderful dress sense, and sometimes she would take me with her when she went to Hackney, to the big shops. We would get on a tram together and she would pay my penny fare and I really thought myself somebody. On the rare occasions when I had managed to save a sixpence, she would leave me at the door of Woolworths and I'd spend a blissful hour choosing my purchase. It was excitement enough to dream about all the week.

Eva worked at the manufacturing chemist in the next street, and we began to hear more and more about the wonderful formulas and cure-alls that were made there. She recommended one special indigestion tablet to yer aunt and uncle, and they swore by it. Aunt would take one, sitting as she always did in the big basement kitchen of her house. Then she would burp loudly, again and again, and if uncle was in, she'd go to the foot of the stairs. "Can you hear me Harry?" Burp, burp, "Wonderful tablets these!" Burp, burp. So Eva's stock really went up, and soon she was able to recommend a corn cure as well.

Even the lav became more interesting, because whereas we had always used neat squares of newspaper, cut up and threaded with string, like everyone else, we now had out of date health catalogues, which were just the right size and better quality than newspaper. What reading there was now! No more need for the *Red Letter* tucked up my jumper, it took me all my time to read about boils and piles and female pills.

When Christmas came, Eva was invited to the firm's dinner. I'd never met anyone who'd been invited to a Dinner Dance and the very idea of dinner at night made my eyes pop. I listened eagerly as Eva discussed her dress with auntie Rosie who, being a court dressmaker, should have really first class ideas on the subject. But her ideas, to Eva's mind, were blooming old fashioned. "She'd have me dress like a flipping schoolkid," she commented bitterly. But the choice was very limited anyway, for being only a few months after Rosie's death, we were in mourning anyway. So she wore a black velvet dress with a white lace collar. She bought a pair of waving tongs and did her hair, too. Even now, the smell of singeing hair brings back the memory of that black velvet dress.

Another milestone came at this time. Auntie Lottie was made manageress of the grocer's where she worked. This meant that they had the flat over the shop rent free. There was a kitchen, a big parlour and two big bedrooms. Such a chance was too good to miss, and so they moved away.

Alas, there was no more Pip Squeak and Wilfred, no more big pocket to take my crusts, and no more trips to Homerton to the Army meetings. How we missed them all! But with their going, and Eva now at work and earning twelve and six a week, we were able to climb the social scale of our little community. Mum decided to keep the whole of the downstairs, and only let the one upstairs room which had been the aunties' bedroom. She had a gas cooker put on the landing outside the room, and had no difficulty in letting this apartment for four shillings weekly.

Our new tenants were a nice young couple, recently married. He was a postman, and they were probably the very first people I got to know who were not relations. They were very quiet, and sometimes they would invite me up to their room, though Mum would stress that I was not to make a nuisance of myself. But Mr Reynolds would sit and play draughts with me, and even taught me how to do a weekly competition in the 'John Bull'. This was called bullets, and we only had to make an apt comment on any phrase on a list. Sometimes, we would come up with a really good one, and Mr Reynolds would pay out the sixpence required and send it in, and we'd dream all next week about what we'd do if our entry won the prize. And what prizes were offered! Sometimes as much as ten shillings a week for life. Though I worried a bit, because if they had all that money coming in, they'd move away and I'd miss them.

The cooking smells were a bit powerful nowadays. If we came in from school and smelt onions, they could be ours, or coming from the landing, if Mrs Reynolds was cooking. And if she was cooking onions and we were having fish, it was a really overwhelming aroma!

I had just started going with Eva to chapel on Sunday mornings then, and I'd walk back thinking about my Sunday dinner. It was blessed to be hungry on a Sunday. It was written in the Bible: 'Blessed are they who hunger and thirst after righteousness, for they shall be filled.' To my mind, I'd qualified on the righteousness bit by going to chapel, and now I was entitled to be hungry and thirsty. To open our front door and smell it all, beef with the fat making splashing noises on the fire oven door and dripping its gravy into the pudding cooking in the tin underneath it, and lamb and mint sauce wafting down the stairs: gosh, it was worth being righteous for!

I don't know what made Eva suddenly take up this morning service lark; I expect she went along because she and her friends had their eyes on a couple of the young fellows who went with their parents, but once I had been with her, nothing could keep me away. I hadn't even realised that anyone could go every week, we at the Sunday School usually went in the church twice a year, on Christmas Sunday and on Anniversary Day.

How we all loved this special day! The whole Sunday School, having practised special hymns over and over again for about ten weeks, would go into the actual church and sit in the gallery, where we filled every seat. Everyone wore a flower in their buttonhole, and it was the day for the wearing of new clothes. New hats and coats for the girls and women, and a new shirt and tie for the men. We always hoped for a fine day, and folk who had moved away would treat the day as one of reunions. Those who had married came back, bringing their babies to show to their friends, and there was a real air of festivity about the place. I loved it all, especially the hymn singing, and when I found I could go and sit downstairs with the grown ups any Sunday I cared to, I took to going along with Eva. She always pushed me off afterwards, for she and her friends went awalking on the Prom, but I didn't mind, and sang all the way home.

I knew Mr and Mrs Reynolds were not poor people, because they had a real gramophone, with lots of records, and none of us had one. Only yer aunt, and she didn't play hers. I had a toy one that played real records, it was probably the most expensive toy I ever possessed. The aunties bought it for me the Christmas after Rosie died, and all the family played it. Even Dad bought a new record for it sometimes, because it was our family music. The records were small, about the size of today's singles, but the latest tunes could be bought in Woolworths for sixpence each. Some of these records I still have. 'I don't care what you used to be, I know what you are today.' 'Paddling Madeline Home' and 'I'll take her back if she wants to come back, the girl that was stolen from me.' I still have the tiny gramophone too, with its little horn and the key to wind it. But in those far off days we played it incessantly, dancing to its jigs and hornpipes.

I used to love sitting by the Reynold's fire, listening to their real gramophone, for they were such nice people. They didn't drink, or even swear, and sometimes they would sit and hold hands by the fireside. Yet they had but one room, all their coal and water had to be carried upstairs and all their dirty water carried down and outside. Today, we would hold up our hands in horror and picture them as real slums. Yet they were not, they were clean and tidy and decent and knew what thousands today never do, the bliss of contentment. They were not engaged in an everlasting struggle to live up to the Jones, but were happy to live together in love.

One morning, I awoke to the sound of strange voices and my tummy lurched. Not more trouble! I padded to the door, to see Mrs Reynolds standing on the landing in her nightie, and old Mrs Horner from round the corner standing talking to her.

"You'll be alright duck," she was saying, "and by the time your Alf gets back, I reckon we'll have good news for him."

Mum came along then, and shoo'd me inside the bedroom "Now you'll be good today and not give me any bother. Mrs Reynolds isn't well and you mustn't make a noise."

Not well? She didn't look ill to me. Not ill enough for Mrs Horner who always went in houses when people had died. She didn't look ill enough for a doctor either, standing there and laughing, like she was. Grown ups were funny. I decided against going to the park even though it was bright and sunny and a school holiday. Something mysterious was happening and I didn't want to miss anything. So I went across the court to call for Renee. She always knew everything, anyway.

I told her about Mrs Reynolds and she just stared at me. "I heard my Mum saying she was late, last night."

"Late for what?" I enquired anxiously, and a slow look of incredulous unbelief came over Renee's peaky face. She pushed her glasses back on her nose.

"You don't mean you don't know? Where's yer eyes gal? The baby, of course. Your lodger's having a baby." Then as she looked at my stunned expression she added, "My Gawd, don't tell me you really didn't know!"

"I didn't know, how could I?" I asked. "The doctor isn't there, and he doesn't always bring one when he comes, anyway." I knew that, to my grief. Several times, when Mum had been queer, I'd pleaded with her to call the doctor. I honestly thought that babies were a sort of consolation prize given occasionally to women who had to stay in bed. As to where they actually came from, I just hadn't a clue. Even the mice had baby mice, appearing overnight by some sort of magic.

I stood open mouthed, while Renee called to Maud who lived next door. "She don't know where babies come from, she really don't know."

I stood before them trembling in my ignorance and Renee took a deep long breath. She was going to enjoy this, actually finding a little innocent who thought that babies came in doctor's black bags.

"Look Dol, you can see she's having a baby. She's all big and fat in front, where the baby is lying in her belly. When her time comes, she gives a wopping great scream and it comes out."

"Splitting her right through," added Maud with relish.

"Then they have to sew her up," finished Renee.

I walked to the corner and stared ahead with unbelieving eyes. It couldn't be true. Renee grabbed my arm. "Look, I'm not lying. Look at Mrs Gibbons, just going up the street. Remember how thin she used to be. Now look at her big fat belly. You'll see, she's only got a week or so to go." I looked at Mrs Gibbons, remembering her as she had been. Mum had been in the habit of calling her "that bean pole".

I went back home and sat on the doorstep, listening anxiously. Only the sound of a bowl clattering on the landing. No doctor, no crying; and thank goodness, no screaming either. Mum was busy in the kitchen; it wasn't likely that Mrs Reynolds was going to split open, otherwise Mum wouldn't have been in the kitchen making meat pie.

After a time, I went back to where Maud and Renee stood giggling together on the corner. There was something else I just had to know. "How does the baby get into the belly in the first place?"

With much shrieking of laughter, Renee caught me by the ear and whispered. Her breath smelled of onions, and the appalling few words she whispered seared through my being.

"Of course they don't — that can't possibly be true!" I shouted in my distress, but there stood Maud, nearly fourteen and knowing everything, just nodding her head.

"Well," I gathered up the remnants of my dignity, "your father and mother might do such awful things, but I'm certain my Mum and Dad don't. They couldn't."

"They just could," laughed Renee heartily, "or you wouldn't be here yourself, you little fool."

Unbidden, my mind flashed back to that Sunday afternoon when Mum and Dad had shouted to me to get out of their bedroom, when Dad had been squashing Mum.

I had to know everything now. "How then does the Mum know when there is a baby growing?"

Renee sat down on the kerb and shook her head. "This kid don't know anything! Don't you even know about periods?"

Miserably, I shook my head and they proceeded to enlighten me. "And if it doesn't happen to you by the time you are fifteen, you die. So it's no good saying you don't want it."

At that moment the doctor arrived, and propping his bike up against our window, he went into the house. Renee was quicker than me and much more daring. She darted across the road and lifted the top of the flapping black bag still on the bike. "No baby in there, is there Dol," she taunted.

After a time, the doctor came downstairs, took the bag off the bike and went into the house. I slipped indoors to where Mum stood at the foot of the stairs. "Get out and play for Christ's sake," she shouted, and then I knew that things were at crisis point, for she didn't often swear at us like that.

A small knot of women had gathered by the corner lamp post now, standing with their arms folded in their aprons. "Poor little devil," sighed auntie Liz, "I thought she'd have it rough. Been hanging about a couple of days already. Reckon he'll send her away if it doesn't come soon."

She flapped her apron at me then and I wandered off, to where Steve was playing cards by himself in the doorway.

"Steve," I demanded, "did you know Mrs Reynolds was having a baby?"

"Sure," he answered. "Everyone knows." "But Steve," I persisted, do you know how babies start?"

"Course I do." His tone was non commital; he was much more interested in his cards. But Steve had taught me so much, I just had to go on. "Do you believe it, Steve?"

"Oh, of course I do. Look, if you're that keen, come up to our room and take your bloomers down and I'll show you."

"No thank you," I replied indignantly. "Don't you think it's the most horrible thing you ever heard?"

"No," he answered, thoughtfully, "not really. Actually, they say it's very nice. Do you want me to show you or not?"

He shuffled the cards together and packed them up. It seemed to me that he was now quite interested. He stood up, hand on the bannister. "Coming?" "No," I answered shortly. Unconsciously female, I drew back now that I had roused him. "I'd much rather you showed me how to castle in chess, like you promised."

"Alright, get the chessmen out." Steve was easy going, like his Dad, and we settled down to a game. When I looked out of the door, the doctor's bike had gone, so I ran home, where Mum greeted me with a big smile. She took me up to Mrs Reynolds' room, where she lay smiling with a lovely little baby girl in her arms.

I longed to ask if she was split open, but didn't dare, either then or later, when she was up and about again.

Before long, I was able to accept this aspect of the facts of life. After all,

I should have known babies came out of mothers. I knew that hens laid eggs, and eggs were only unborn chickens. Once again, it was Sunday School and Bible teaching that came to my aid.

'Once in royal David's City' explained it all.

'Where a mother laid her baby.' It was the same really, except that a mother hatched the egg before she laid it. Hens laid it while it was still an egg.

Now I began to notice when the mice grew fat, in fact, you could prod them a bit and feel the baby mice inside. It was quite interesting to look for fat women when we went shopping and I watched carefully at the baby linen shop to see how many of the window gazers were having babies.

But the other fact...No. It was out. Why, Mum grumbled when I put my hankie in my bloomers pocket and pulled it out in front of Dad. "Don't lift your frock up in front of your father. It isn't nice."

Only once a year did Dad inspect us thoroughly. That was when we had our new combinations in the autumn. How I hated combs! Thick wool and cotton, with legs and sleeves and high necks, buttoned all down the front and with a big vent at the back so that we could manage without taking the things off every time we went to the lav. The combs went over our woollen vests, under our bloomers and petticoats. No wonder 'liberty bodices' were so named, when they became fashionable and took the place of the hated combs.

Our under petticoat was of flannel, then we had a flannelette one, beautifully feather stitched all round, and on top of this, a cambric one, with twice as much feather stitching and a lace edging.

When we went into this winter gear, usually round about bonfire night, Mum would show Dad how well the new combs fitted and we would bend over to let him see that they were not slack, to rub, or too tight, to cut under our legs.

Once this yearly inspection was over, Dad steered clear of us and our bodies, he even stayed out while we were bathed in front of the kitchen fire.

When we were older, we had our bath night when Mum and Dad went to the pictures. Mum would carry in the buckets of hot water from the kitchen copper before they went out, and we would have our bath, both using the same water, and then bath the dog too, if she needed it. Then we carried all the water outside and emptied it into the yard.

I used to think it must be awful to have a bathroom and not be able to sit by a big fire to have my bath. The only bathroom I ever saw was the one at yer aunt's, cold and grim and all white paint. I never saw her use it either, she used to take a kettle of hot water into her bedroom to wash at the big marble washstand. It was much more sensible to bath by the fire.

Dad and Mum had theirs after we had gone to bed, and Mum would hang Dad's clean long pants and vest on the armchair by the fire, so that he could get into them all nice and warm.

If the night was very cold, Dad would take the shelf out of the fire oven, all hot and almost glowing red, wrap it in several thicknesses of upholstery velvet, and put it in his bed. Sometimes, if the weather was really bitter, he would take a huge shovel full of glowing coals and go belting up the stairs and put them in the bedroom fireplace, smoke and smuts following him in a great cloud. We had stone hot water bottles, not much comfort to cuddle, but at least they took the icy chill off the bottom of the bed, though mine invariably fell out of bed in the night with a great thump and woke us all up.

Eight

The new baby upstairs flourished, but before long, her parents were looking for a bigger place. I cried when they left us, although the new lodger had a big belly when they arrived and it was not long before there was another new baby in the house.

Dad was not so keen on these people though. The woman called Dad "old bean," and would even come through our kitchen when we were having a meal, a thing that Mrs Reynolds would never do.

"Just going to get some water," she'd say gaily. "Hope you're going to leave some of that dinner old bean, it smells ever so good to me." And she'd come up to the table, and sometimes laughingly pick a potato from Dad's plate, while we looked up in frozen horror, wondering at the woman's daring.

For a couple of months, she got away with it too, but one day, she went too far. If she'd have had any sense, she'd have realised that when Dad didn't come in whistling, he was in a bad mood, but it didn't matter to her that he was in one of his very quiet moods, just looking for someone or something to start on. Even the dog kept out of his way on such occasions, you needed to be really thick not to know Dad's moods.

We were all sitting in silence eating our dinner, when in she came, bouncing across the room with her water jug. Her "Hello," was greeted with a glare, but as she returned with her water, she had the nerve to tip Dad's cap forward over his eyes as she passed his chair.

"Cheer up, old bean," she laughed, and wondered what had hit her. Dad leapt to his feet, called her all the names he could lay his tongue to, and using all the words we were not allowed to say, he told her to get out and find new lodgings by the end of the week. "I'll swing first, before I'll let you stay," he bellowed. Then of course, he turned on Mum. She'd let the low down common bitch take the room, she should have seen what she was.

The little family moved out at the end of the week, and Dad vowed we'd have no more lodgers. He'd manage to give Mum another half a dollar and we'd keep the house. A whole house, with no lodgers! I couldn't wait to get to school and boast about it. Lots of my friends were the lodgers and only had a couple of upstairs rooms, but I knew of no one who had the whole house.

Eva was delighted too, because this meant she had a bedroom to herself.

A whole room! Gwen and I shared the big end room, and we talked for hours about what we would do with it. We even bought several pounds of macaroni, painted it all in different colours, broke the long sticks up into little pieces and made a long bead curtain for the window. It looked most artistic too.

Auntie Liz laughed at us. "I suppose you fancy your bloody selves now," she teased over the fence. Well, what if we did. We had something to boast about, anyway. Mum went down Roman Road and bought some new curtaining. Heavy crettone, with big bold flowers all over it. She hesitated a bit, because the pattern was not printed all the way through, and the stall keeper groused. "What do you expect for a tanner a yard," he moaned, "bloody gold thread? You wouldn't get it if I hadn't nicked it." We laughed at that, because they always said they'd pinched the stuff, even within the hearing of a copper. Anyway, Mum bought it, and it never wore out. She gave me some of it, during the war, and even now, my cat reclines on a cushion made from the stuff.

There was another bonus to our occupying the whole house. We were now able to have gas in our bedrooms instead of candles. Before this, we had not been allowed to use upstairs gas, as it came off the lodger's meter, but now Dad bought gas fittings and we had real mantles and proper lights in the bedrooms. Mum even looked at stair carpet, but Dad would have none of it.

"Enough's enough," he growled. "How would you keep it clean? Tell me that. How would you scrub the stairs?" So we had new lino and made do, but it was lovely anyway.

I was glad of the light in the bedroom, because now the Junior County scholarship loomed ahead. This event, predecessor of the Eleven Plus, was held twice yearly. The successful candidates went to grammar school, called secondary school at that time. But not many children were successful, because most of the places were taken up by paying pupils, and only a dozen or so scholarships were available at each school. So the competition was fierce, and any school which managed as many as three scholarships at any one time, really had a feather in its cap.

The names of the successful ones were painted on a big roll of honour hung in the school hall, and it had been my ambition to see my name there for as long as I could remember.

Dad put the pressure on, it was mental arithmetic with my tea and an essay afterwards. Train sums were his speciality. If a train travelling at forty miles an hour leaves Liverpool at ten and passes another travelling in the opposite direction at thirty miles an hour and having left London ten minutes earlier...so on and so on, until I felt I could work out the train timetables for the whole country. Compound interest, fractions, decimals and percentages, I did them all.

I read recently that a comprehensive school Headmaster found one of these Junior County papers and set it to his whole school, the youngest of whom was older than I was when I sat the paper. Only one child out of the thousand would gave gained a grammar school place on the results and two hundred could not answer a single question!

I wonder why? I suppose intelligence alters over the years. When I listen to children in T.V. quizzes such as 'Top of the Form' I know I was not bright as these children are. They astound me with their knowledge. Yet when I recently told a group of nine year olds that I would give a sweet to the first one who told me what nine eights were, they could not answer. Perhaps mental arithmetic is an out of date subject. They have calculating machines and machines to give change in shops, but how will these children know that they are getting a fair deal in the supermarkets of the future?

I have been bulk buying recently as a means of saving on grocery bills, but you need to be able to calculate to find out if an article is worth buying in bulk, for some things are not. Maybe money is becoming so valueless that it doesn't matter what you pay, as long as you get what you want. I know that money in a purse just melts, which is why I've bought a big freezer! Today's young worker asks for ridiculous rises because he just does not understand the value of money.

Anyway, came the Saturday of the Junior County and away I went with my pen and pencil and rubber and ruler and came home feeling quite pleased with myself. Dad's train sum had a place in the problem paper, so he was as pleased as punch. "If you get it, my girl, you'll have your Dad to thank," he purred. And get it I did. He gave me ten bob, the very first time I had owned a piece of paper money. I rushed into the street with it, singing at the top of my voice, "I've got a money note, I've got a money note." I bought a leather case with the money, and Dad put my initials on it.

Now there were schools to be considered and places to apply to. Dad and Mum had to go and see the school Head, and I was eventually fixed up with a place in Clapton. Dear old Laura Place, or the John Howard School for Girls, to give it its rightful name. There was a grant with the scholarship too. Nine pounds a year. Nine whole pounds! I could hardly believe it, and floated on air for a while, until we came down to the brass tacks of buying my brown school uniform. Everything was so dear, and couldn't be bought in Roman Road. It all had to be just so, and even auntie Rosie couldn't run up something that looked near enough.

Added to this, was the cost of my bus fare every day, a penny each way, and three and six per term for the use of plate, glass and cutlery at the school mealtable. There was no suggestion of school dinners of course, only the paying pupils could afford them.

Now life took on a new meaning and was entirely different. Not even the holidays were the same as the elementary schools, and we had every Wednesday afternoon free. Mum used to take me out sometimes, and I really loved it, looking forward to getting home and hearing her say, "Now then, where shall we go today?"

I had to get out each morning soon after eight to catch a bus, and what a business this was. No one then had ever heard of queuing for a bus, so we all just stood where we were and hoped the bus would pull up just in the right spot. The young fellows stood round the corner from the bus stop and jumped on as the bus slowed down to round the corner. Sometimes, I would stand there too, and pray hard that the policeman would hold the bus up just as it got there, so that I too could jump on, but this wasn't often the case, and sometimes I would get shoved and pushed about for nearly half an hour before I managed to get on. There was one nice conductor though, who would let me stand under the stairs, even when the bus was full, and I just loved those mornings. It was easier to get on when it rained hard, because lots of people wouldn't go on top in the rain. But I chanced it, and sat with the canvas cover over my knees and the brim of my hat turned down all round. I think queues were about the best thing to come out of the war!

Going to the school in Clapton gave me one nasty shock. I wasn't so wonderful as I thought I was! There were girls around who could do arithmetic as fast as I, and even faster, and sadly enough, most of these girls were Jewish and learnt Hebrew and somehow found it much easier than I did to grasp German, which was the compulsory other language.

The teachers didn't think I was very wonderful either. I remember the shame of being hauled up in front of the whole form for saying "we was." "Oh, was we," taunted the girls when we got outside, and one of them looked at me as though I was something the cat had dragged in. "You come from Bethnal Green, don't you?" she asked and turned to her friends. "I don't know what this school is coming to!"

I pulled up my long brown stockings and made faces at them, but I didn't do too well on this score either. I wasn't very big for my age, and a couple of girls were real bullies; before the first month was over I was bitterly disillusioned with the whole affair, and didn't like this grand school one bit. Not that I'd admit it at home. I made out that it was all one glorious adventure. I was half scared of the teachers too, for they wore long black robes over their dresses most of the time, except for the gym mistress who wore a little gym slip and looked like a girl. I thought she was rather wonderful, and used to dream that she would fall as she vaulted over the horse, and that I would rush to save her. Of course, I would get injured in the process, but they would all crowd round and say, "Oh, Mousie Clark, you saved her life!"

They had soon found a nickname for me. I talked so much about the mice, indeed they were my only claim to fame. I sold some too, for a time, but got such a belting for selling two males as a breeding pair that I got choked off the idea. My customer came up breathing fire at me, having waited in vain for her mice to be lucrative. "My brother came home from boarding school, this weekend," she said, "and he says those mice are both males. Are you scared I'll pinch all your trade?" She gave me such a hammering that I never dared sell any more mice at school, but the name stuck. After all, I couldn't tell which was which, and I had asked Steve. He held the mice up by their tails for ages before he decided, but apparently even he could make a mistake.

Eventually we all settled down and made our own friends, and by the time the term ended I was happy enough. One of my friends was a big girl who had been particularly spiteful to me at the beginning. For some unknown reason she took me under her wing. If anyone tried to hit me, she'd stand there bristling. "If anyone wants to hit Mousie Clark, they must come to me first," she'd shout and soon my tormentors would go away, for no one wanted a brush with her.

She lived in Stepney, near Chinatown, and told lurid tales about having seen a Chinaman chop another one's head off on the kerb. We never dared say we didn't believe her, either.

My real friend was Gladys, known to us all affectionately as Cutlets. There was something about Cutlets that I loved, right from the start of our schooldays, and now, nearly fifty years later, things are still the same between us. Life has been kind and generous to me, and hard beyond belief to her, but she is still the same kind and gentle soul I met at that big school. If most of us had had half Cutlet's troubles, we'd have succumbed long ago. Dear blind friend of mine, you made that school for me.

During the long school holidays I forgot all my posh friends, and within a few days I was back in the park, or playing the old games in the street. Children don't seem to play these street games any more, but I suppose the streets are too dangerous. But they don't play in the playground either, as we did. They prefer to stay in the Hall at playtime and hold disco sessions, which really means mooning about in a darkened room growing old before their time.

There were so many skipping games we played, chanting as we turned the rope. Slow skips and bumps, which meant two fast turns of the rope between each jump. We sang out, 'Old mother Mason broke her basin, how much did it cost,' then came the fast jumps, 'penny, tuppence, threepence' and so on. There were long slow skips too. Goodness knows where the words had their origin, but we all knew them.

All last night and the night before,
Two Tom cats came knocking at the door.
I went downstairs to let them in
And they hit me on the head with the rolling pin.
The rolling pin was made of glass,
They knocked me over and snacked my...wheeeeee.

We never said the last word, but just laughed and ran from the rope.

There was

Handy pandy sugar de candy, french and almond rock.
Bread and butter for your supper, that's all your mother's got.

A great favourite was, 'Rosy apple, lemonade tart, tell me the name of your sweetheart,' and then there were innumerable questions. 'What does his name begin with?' And we'd go through the alphabet until we were out. Then, 'Will he marry me. Yes, No, Yes No.' Next time round. 'What will you wear? Silk, satin, cotton, rags.' Finally, 'How will you get to the wedding? Car, carriage, wheelbarrow, dung cart.' This game took hours to play.

As well as the skipping rhymes, there were the dipping ones, when we had to decide who should take the rope end, or hide first in hide-and-seek. Our favourite was 'Tinky pinky, pen and ink, I smell a nasty stink, it must be you.' Unquestionably the law of the Medes and Persians, this one.

Every game had its season. There were whips and tops. The peg of the top was stuck firmly between the kerbstone and paving stone, and whipped away with a nice piece of cord on a stick. We could keep that top going up and down the smooth asphalted roadway for about twenty minutes.

The boys played marbles in the gutter, with one special glarney stone and a lot of plain ones. The greatest prize was a ball bearing, which was worth almost a dozen marbles.

We all played blowsy, even the girls. It was merely a question of putting down a cigarette card, picture side down, on the window sill, to be covered by the opponent's card. We then took turns to blow, and every card we blew picture side up, we won. The bigger boys stood half a dozen cards at the time on edge, and competition was fierce among them.

What children these days play fivestones, or gobs-and-bonsters as we called it? Occasionally, I have seen children playing a similar game called jacks, but it hasn't the intricate movement of fivestones, with its 'backsie', and 'treble stone', which we played on the pavement.

When we tired of playing, we would sit by the wall and play guessing games, or watch the writing in the sky. So often on summer evenings a high plane would drone overhead and write, usually 'Oxo' or 'Daily Mail', in vapour trails across the evening sky. Even the Mums would come out to watch this fascinating performance.

We collected pins too, though what we did with them besides count to see who had the most, I can't recall. Putting a lot of little treasures in a fancy box, we would stand on the corner and call out. 'Pin for a look and a jolly good look.' One girl achieved a wonderful store of pins after an operation on her leg. We all wanted a peep at that shocking scar.

Another version of the same game, was to put paper squares from chocolates between the leaves of a book. Beautifully smoothed and carefully placed, these small foil squares were greatly prized. 'Pin for a pick and a jolly good pick,' we'd call.

Of course, there were the dare games, but we didn't often take part in these, only watch with bated breath while the boys tied a thin strong string to a door knocker, when it was almost dark, carry it across the road and fasten the other end to the opposite knocker. Then they'd knock, and run away and hide. The opening door would cause the opposite knocker to lift, and when the irate householder closed his door, the other knocker would fall and the whole thing was repeated. Occasionally this went on for several minutes, the mystified occupants getting madder and madder as they crouched behind their door, hoping to catch the tormentor. Why this game was called 'Knocking Down Ginger' I never could find out.

Another dare game was quite simple, but not always plain sailing. We had to go into every shop, from our bakers, right up to the chemists, about fifteen shops in all, and ask for something at every one. All the shops were open until eight and nine on Saturdays, and the poor weary shopkeeper was not very keen on kids coming in and asking for something she didn't sell. My cousin always asked "How much a dozen are the penny eggs?" or, "Do you stock tea in ounce packets?" I used to say, "Please have you any empty boxes, about nine inches square?" which worked, even in the pawn. I stated a size so that I wouldn't get laden with boxes before I was half way through.

Our favourite indoor game was 'Dead Man's Dark Scenery' and again, I haven't a clue as to where it got this name. Dividing into two teams, one side would go into another room, and the remaining ones would cover up one, two, or even three of their number with all the coats. How hot it was, lying motionless beneath all the coats! Then making sure they had left no peepholes, the others would leave the room, yelling as they did so, 'Dead Man's Dark Scenery,' disguising their voices if they could because the first ones would listen hard to the call.

Now it was their turn, to rush into the room and try to guess who was under the coats. No touching was allowed, but it was permissible to try and make the hidden ones laugh, once movement had been discovered. Then there would be a yell for the hidden ones, called by name, to arise, and a correct guess meant a change of sides.

We spent hours playing this game, leaving false clues like a wrong shoe sticking out a little, or a big ball to look like an extra head. It was great fun and any number could join in.

The new school continued to be interesting, now that I had settled down and I used to go out even earlier each morning, because the very first covered buses were now on the roads, and there was one on our route just after eight. I loved to boast that I'd been on a covered top bus. My other favourite bus was a pirate bus, a bright purple vehicle numbered 525. This did not belong to the General Bus Co., and the driver would madly overtake all the other buses, collecting all the passengers he could. The conductor would stack us in until we could hardly breathe, and never used the hateful words "Full right up." I was never late for school when he was around.

Our longest bus rides were to the dentist. Mum had no faith in school clinics and felt that we must have the best as far as she was able. So every three or six months, she took us to the Royal Dental Hospital in Leicester Square; and how I hated it!

Somehow, when people talk today about dental health, I wonder just how much tooth decay is due to too many sweets, or lack of brushing, or fluoride in the water. We all went to the same dentist, had the same food and used the same toothpowder, yet every visit was the same. Nothing wrong with my sisters' teeth, but a load of work to be done on mine. So by the time I was twenty three, I was well equipped with dentures, while my sisters still have their own teeth.

It was the students who did the work, though my mother fondly saw them all as highly qualified, and I'm afraid they didn't take the work as it came. I would sit there on the long hard bench with about twenty other folk, watching them all working and try to guess which one would do my fillings. My name always seemed to be called out by the one I least liked the look of! The kindly looking chaps would sift through the cards and when they pushed one to the back of the pile, I took a guess that that was mine!

Eventually I would be called, sit in the dreaded chair with my mouth open; and the student would start to grind and grind away, his foot working hard on the pedal. When he felt he had done enough, he would call the supervisor, usually the same elderly, thin faced man with goldrimmed glasses, a mass of grey hair and a wicked looking pick in his hand. He would poke and prod and bring tears to my eyes, while I sat and gripped the arms of the chair, not daring to make a fuss, since my sisters were sitting with Mum, waiting to go home. How I longed to join the happy ranks of those who, going to sit in the inspection chair would hear those magic words, "Nothing this time, make an appointment for six months time." But in all the years I went there, it was never my good fortune. No one ever thought of injections for fillings in those days!

Having a tooth out by gas was even worse. We all sat together in a big waiting room, men separated from women by a big wooden partition, but children with adults. A big notice advised us to loosen all corsets and tight clothing and to go to the W.C. I used to sit and wonder whether I ought to unbutton my combs. I went to the lav as advised, but the wait was so long that I was waiting to go again, yet dare not, since my name might get called while I was outside. The children were usually left till last, perhaps because their teeth were easier to pull when the students were tired. I sat watching women go in, all smiles, and come back with blood dripping from their tightly shut mouths. Twenty or more teeth at a time were commonplace extractions, and I lived in mortal dread that they might not remember to stop at one or two when I went in!

Auntie Lottie used to tell me though, how lucky we were to have a real dentist to go to. At the turn of the century, when she was a girl, there was a monthly clinic held at a church hall in Bethnal Green. Anyone who had bad toothache could go there, line up and have the bad tooth pulled out. No gas, no injections and no painkillers. One day, a neighbour asked Auntie Lottie to line up and mind her place in the queue while she popped indoors for a minute. Lottie stood in the line and got nearer and nearer to the front and the neighbour, who had probably got cold feet by this time, failed to return.

Poor little Lottie reached the front. "Open wide," snapped the dentist, and even as she opened her mouth to explain the situation, her head was forced back, a gag inserted and two teeth pulled out! "I suppose they were bad, anyway," laughed auntie, telling us the tale, "but you ought to be grateful to your mother, looking after you, the way she does."

I suppose I was, but the only enjoyment for me was the trip we made afterwards, if there was time, to the National Gallery to look at the paintings. Perhaps that wasn't a good idea really, because always to associate paintings with toothache, is not exactly a child's guide to the pleasures of artistic appreciation. However, Mum liked to get her money's worth, and having paid threepence fare to get up to Leicester Square, she liked to get as much as she could.

After Janet and the aunties moved to Knightsbridge, we had another opportunity to take a long bus ride. How we loved to get on top of a bus and ride all that way!

After I went to the grammar school, Mum used to let us go alone to visit. If I was old enough to go on one bus without an adult, then I was old enough to go on another! Occasionally, we stayed a couple of days with the aunties. We would talk about this holiday for weeks beforehand; Gwen making new clothes for her doll, complete outfits of neat stitchery, while I got by with a new bit of ribbon tied around mine.

We were left very much to our own devices in Knightsbridge, and we'd walk into Harrods, chins in the air and hands tightly clenched, wander across to the lift and ask for the third floor, trying hard to pretend we were somebodies. If we were asked what we wanted, I would come out with the formula I used at home, "Have you any empty boxes about nine inches square please?" They never had, but would politely suggest that we tried another department, probably laughing up their sleeve at the two little girls with scruffy dolls, walking around their lovely store.

Once, we bumped into a lady, being handed in at the door as we left, bows and gracious smiles all round. "That," breathed the doorman, "is the Queen of Spain."

The museums were a world of wonder too. If it was wet, one of the aunties would hurry us across the road and into the Victoria and Albert Museum at about two o'clock and tell us to stay there until five. Then auntie Rosie would call for us on her way home from work.

I always thought her shop a funny place. It had about six windows, but with only one dress in each. Silly really, when there was room for about twenty. The prices were mad, for who would pay 50 guineas for one dress!

Most of all, we enjoyed the 'Dead Zoo', which was our name for the Natural History Museum, and it was no hardship to be left there for the afternoon. If Steve was with us, then we went a bit further afield to the Science Museum, where we organised a competition to see who could find the most buttons to press. Not that I ever looked at the models with any intelligence, but I loved to press the buttons and see things moving. After the little shop closed at eight o'clock, we were allowed to play there, and had fun playing shops with real goods and money.

"Please have you any empty boxes, about nine inches square?"

Surprisingly, the people who frequented auntie's little shop, were no better off than the people we knew. They bought little bits and pieces like two ounce packets of tea and a quarter of butter, and there was the same stiff notice about not asking for credit.

There, just behind Harrods, were the little people without decent shoes, who had only oil lamps instead of gas like we had, and who would ask for a rasher of bacon. Indeed, their houses were not a patch on ours, with paint peeled doors and tatty broken windows.

Nostalgia took me down that street, not long ago. It had the quiet air of a Kensington Mews, the houses had wrought iron gates, electric coach lamps hung in the porchways; and the little Row bathed in the glow of having come up in the world. And so it had, for it has become a fashionable place to live. One of the houses was for sale, its price was thirty seven thousand pounds, yet when Lottie traded there, the place was let at a rental of ten shillings a week.

After they moved away from us, the aunties too came up in the world. With no fares and no rent to pay, they blossomed out and bought themselves fur coats. When they came to see us, it was like having rich relations come to visit and their coats smelt of moth balls, just like yer aunt's did. They came for Christmas too, and uncle Will said we'd have to tone things down a bit, if they were staying; and we couldn't treat them like one of the family any more.

I loved Christmas when the family were all together. Uncle would sit looking at a photo of himself in soldier's uniform, which hung in pride of place on the parlour wall, and several times during the evening, he would rise slowly to his feet, glass in hand, and call for silence.

"Stand up straight, Jean, shoulders back Steve. Put your dolly down Gwen. Everyone, please be uprising."

We would all stand up, even Mum and Dad, and uncle would say solemnly, "The King, gawd bless him." Then we would all sit down again, and Dad and he would go on with the funny songs and ditties that only came out at Christmas. We owned a real gramophone now, and it was not an old fashioned one with a horn either. Dad had records of the old music hall songs and we joined in them all. 'Daisy Daisy,' and 'Beer beer, glorious beer,' being top favourites. Only Mum refused to sing. Dad once offered her ten bob to sing just one verse solo, but she refused. Something died in her, when Rosie died, and she was never quite the same. But all in all, Christmases were hilarious affairs.

Sometimes, Gwen and I would go outside for a few minutes, just to hear all the pianos going honky tonk, up and down the street. With 'Knees up Mother Brown' in one house and 'It's a long way to Tipperary' next door, it was a lovely sound, especially as everyone had got sweating hot and all the windows were open. Sometimes a fight would break out and spill out into the street, but someone would throw a jug of water over the participants and that soon cooled things down. Most families had one member at least who could knock out a tune on the old pianos, or, like us, they aspired to a gramophone, and it was music all the way.

On New Year's Eve, they had another party in most houses; but even if they didn't, all the doors would open as the train whistles blasted and the factory hooters sounded, and the women would come out into the street banging on an old tin tray, yelling 'Happy New Year'.

The noise would wake us, if we were in bed, and we'd rush to the windows and shout out in unison with everyone else. Those who'd been drinking would dance in the street, but everyone was happy, even if they were out of work and hardly knew where the next meal was coming from. Who could tell...maybe the New Year would be the one to change their luck. If wishes could help, then things would go well, sure enough.

Stephen thought he could tell a 'he' mouse from a 'she'.

Nine

Eva was really growing up now. Gwen and I used to tease her a lot, and looking back, I think she had a lot to put up with. She had the unfortunate knack of rubbing Dad up the wrong way, and now there were more rows than ever. She'd come in at night, after we were in bed, and we'd hear the ominous sounds of things being thrown about and Dad losing his temper. When she had gone up to bed, still tearfully standing up for herself, Dad would, as always, start on Mum, blaming her for the way she had brought us up.

How I wished she would learn to take the line of least resistance as I did, and keep out of his way. I remember once breaking off one of his carnation buds with my ball. I froze in horror as I realised it was his special, a beautiful white flower tipped with rosy pink. Every evening he had gone straight outside to look at it, ever since it had been a newly formed bud. And now, the fat, pink-tinged beauty lay forlornly on the earth! With scarlet face and trembling fingers, I looked guiltily around, picked it up and flushed it quickly down the lav.

The storm was smouldering when I went in, after rushing out to the street to play, but it was nearly bedtime and I didn't wait to be asked if I'd seen the flower. I hurried up to bed with a book.

It's hard to hold a post mortem without a body, so discounting dogs and cats, who would at least have left the bud, Dad could only blame one of his own pigeons. He stood looking at them all in the loft and I think he felt like slitting all their crops to find the guilty party!

I was not normally a deceitful child, but if deceit would save a row, then I didn't have any qualms. I even saved up a sixpence and bought a packet of Gold Flake cigarettes, the brand Dad always smoked. He would sometimes leave a sixpence on the mantlepiece when he went upstairs for a nap, telling Eva to go and get him some before he woke up. Then, if she forgot, or didn't bother, I'd put the cigarettes on the shelf and take the sixpence ready for the next time. Anything to save a row.

Gwen and I had another excitement now though, because our big sister had a young man. They were not boyfriends in those days, but real 'young men' who came courting. They would walk in the park, up and down the Prom, and we would follow, at a discreet distance. When they came to a road, even a little one, he would take her elbow and steer her across, as though the poor thing couldn't manage the smallest step on her own!

She started attending chapel absolutely regularly now and we, not to be outdone, followed suit. Three times every Sunday, so that Mum and Dad thought they'd got a family of religious maniacs on their hands.

The young man was the chapel organist, and Eva would take her place in the gallery, so that he could come and sit with her during the sermon. His father and mother belonged to the chapel too, and his father was Sunday School Superintendent. His auntie was my Sunday School teacher, and this gave me a real thrill. For in a roundabout way, I was now one of the people I had always envied, a member of a family who really belonged to the place, instead of just one of the kids who came to the Sunday School. After all, if Eva married into this elite family, I'd have relations, in a distant way, at the chapel. It came to me with a shock, that I'd always been jealous of the girl I'd fought with on the first day, because she belonged!

I realised suddenly too, that Sunday School teachers didn't get paid for their work. They just did it, for love of God. It shook me, and I stopped putting toffee papers on the old dear's hat, and saying 'sausage' whenever I came to a word beginning with S in the Bible. I ceased singing 'without a shirt' on the end of every line of some of the hymns, as I had always done for a laugh. My favourite had always been a chorus. 'They shall run and not be weary, they shall walk and not faint.' 'Without a shirt' fitted in marvelously with this hymn.

I envied Eva, and when the family invited us all to tea, Mum and Dad as well, I knew that things were getting serious. The Brown family didn't drink, they said Grace before every meal, and they had a little organ in their parlour. After tea, Mrs Brown played hymns on this, and we all joined in, except Mum and Dad. Sitting there must have been a real ordeal for Dad, poor man.

Duty done, they didn't ask us again as a family, but if ever Gwen or I called there, we were made most welcome. I discovered that there was to be a scripture exam at the Sunday School, and this was right up my street. The lessons were to be held at the Brown house, and every week, I went there for lessons, and Eva didn't like it one bit, for Mrs Brown asked me to stay to tea. Eva accused me of going to spy, but it was not so. How could I explain what it was I found there? I didn't really know myself, it was an intangible atmosphere that I could never have described, but I used to think up innumerable excuses to call. Mrs Brown was always laughing, she had an infectious almost childish laugh that giggled; she called her husband dear, and neither of them ever swore. When Mr Brown said 'Christ' he really meant the Son of God. Theirs was the first Christian home I had ever been in and it made a profound impression on me. They not only attended chapel three times on Sundays, but they went along to a Bible study on Wednesdays and a prayer meeting on Saturdays. I never even knew before, that these last named were public meetings, but now I shyly crept in occasionally on a Saturday evening, to listen to Mr Brown praying in his rich Yorkshire brogue. They had only the one son, and it seemed to me that they doted on the little teenager he was all set to marry.

How Eva managed it, I shall never know, but Mum and Dad bought a piano. Not a honky tonk old Joanna, but a lovely new piano. Now, when Jim came to our house, he sat and played. Chopin, Wagner, Beethoven, names I had never heard of and didn't even pronounce correctly, Jim sat and played on our lovely new piano; and I longed to have the windows open so that the neighbours could hear the real music which came from our house. Eva started having music lessons and Jim and she sat for ages in the front room alone, with only the occasional few bars of music from time to time. But apart from these spells, she was never at home and she never came in next door with us, for she didn't see fit to introduce Jim to them all.

She started going to Oxford Street now, to buy her clothes, and really thought she was somebody. After all, we had always thought of Selfridges as somewhere to look in the window, not actually to buy from.

My cousin Will was courting too, and often when we went in, his girl was spending the evening there. Nothing highbrow about Phyllis. She stood up one evening singing the latest song, 'Oh, do, do, do, do, something.' She swayed in front of Will as she sang, hands on his shoulders and big eyes tempting him. 'Oh, do, do something.' So he did. He seized a plate of red jelly from the table and put it down the front of her blouse, the red staining the yellow silk. How she shrieked, and how we laughed, as she swore and carried on at him. No, she wasn't in the same class as my sister.

When I looked at Eva walking up the street with her young man, in his neat suit and with a rolled umbrella, I felt a sudden swift compassion for her, and wished we could move away. To live somewhere else, where people didn't know everyone else's business and didn't make rude comments. 'Stuck up little bitch,' they would call to each other, as Eva and Jim walked arm in arm.

My grammar school uniform didn't help either; and I too was called stuck up. I was stuck up maybe, but under it, I was getting desperately anxious, for I still half heartedly believed what Renee had told me. If I didn't start my periods soon, I was heading for an early grave! I didn't want to die, and snooping around, I found that most of my school friends had started. There were two envelopes in the school gym, and if swimming lessons were missed for this legitimate reason, then our name must be put in the envelope. I watched my friends going to the gym and missing swimming, and I seriously thought about making my will. Not that I had much to leave, but I didn't want them all fighting over my goods. So I divided things out, leaving my Sunday School Bible to Mr Brown, who could make best use of it, and as my fifteenth birthday approached, I waited to die.

The dreaded birthday passed and nothing happened to me and I changed my fear. Renee was wrong maybe, but what if I was so good that I was heading for a virgin birth? Maybe I was having a baby and didn't know it! After all, I bet the Virgin Mary was dead scared when she found out, and no one, absolutely no one, would have believed her tale, especially her Mum! My relief when I found I was normal after all, surpassed all my wildest hopes! Now I was ordinary like my friends, and the following swimming day sent me on winged feet into the gym envelopes.

Growing older, I was badly in need of more money, for the twopence pocket money from Dad and the twopence from Mum, didn't go very far. So I took to baby minding on a bigger scale. The bakers were glad to have me take their baby off their hands for the day on Saturday, and would give me a shilling. "Sweated labour," Dad called it, for I'd take the baby, in its posh pram, before nine o'clock on a Saturday morning, bring it back and help get its bottle at lunch time, rush home and eat my own dinner and take it back to the park from about two until six. Then I'd help get it ready for bed.

That shilling was worth having, and further more, the bakers had their very own car. A little red Austin Seven; and they sometimes took me out with them. It was the very first car I had ever been in! I'd have minded the baby for nothing to get that car ride!

Eva started on again about moving, and every few days she'd say something to Mum, and Mum would show Dad the Saturday paper with all the advertisements about houses. All around us, estates were going up in Essex, and we'd dream of a future outside Bethnal Green. On my afternoons off from school, we'd take a train to Buckhurst Hill and actually walk into the new houses, planning where we'd put things, if they were really ours. For six hundred pounds, we could get a detached three bedroomed house, with a square hall and little round window in it. Long gardens...side entrances, how many of those houses, now on sale in the fiftyfive thousand range, did we try to own in those early thirties! But Dad was adamant. The pigeons were his latest excuse, for they were not allowed in many of the new areas.

I didn't realise I was getting snobby myself, until one of my friends invited me to her house. The furnishings were not so good as ours, and the house itself not much better, but no one sat outside the front door on an old chair in her road, and no one called out rude comments when we walked to her gate. Neither did her front door open directly onto the pavement. Her Dad was a policeman and I never saw him sharpen a match to pick his teeth with as my Dad did, and he didn't wear his cap in the house all the time, or spit in the fire.

So many things I had always accepted, now seemed to me to be wrong, what with the Brown family, where we used table napkins rolled up in silver rings, and the girls at school who lived in Hackney or Dalston.

Mr Brown had a big influence on other girls besides us, for he often found jobs for them, especially school leavers. He had a friend in the City who owned an underwear factory, and like himself, this man was also a Christian. When he needed staff, he just asked Mr Brown and the factory was kept supplied with learners from our Sunday School. Gwen and Jean were now coming up to fourteen and both had their eyes on a job in the Holborn factory. I wasn't too happy about this because my father had signed papers for me to stay on at school until sixteen at the least and I was now half heartedly studying for matric. I say half heartedly, because things were pretty bad in the employment world at this time. Men who had jobs in 1932, hung on to them for grim death and the two million who were out of work were always waiting to step into their shoes. So when short time work started for Dad and there was less money coming into the house, Mum looked around for ways and means to add a bit. No more lodgers, that was certain, for Dad said he'd swing first, but money was really very tight.

Gwen started work at the Holborn factory and I felt, for the very first time, that she and I were drifting apart. We had always done things together; and when she offered me a threepence pocket money, I felt dreadful. I was afraid she would gang up on me with Eva, who kept making comments about me being kept as a lady, by her. I howled my eyes out and prayed that something might come along. And so it did. Dad's work was cut to half time, and Mum went to the school asking that they be relieved of their obligation to keep me there. So, I entered my last term, only nine months away from matric, tore to shreds my dreams of going on to college and becoming a teacher, and began to write stories instead. Having lost heart in work, since I had no goal, I devised a smashing scheme. I'd write a lurid love story, loan it out to my friends in exchange for their prep books, and copy all their work, writing out long equations and theorems which meant absolutely nothing to me whatsoever.

Chapel began to mean more to me than anything else now, because I not only had the Browns, I also had Father Christmas!

I had been helping organise the infants' party, when I met up with him. He was a recent member of the church, whom I had never met before. Somehow, I was amused by the fact that this man had a bowler hat, and when he left his things in a neat pile to dress up as Father Christmas, I took and hid the bowler hat in the pulpit. The church was dark and solemn, and I stood in the silence and listened to God.

It always seemed to me that God was very near, in that quiet and deserted chapel building. Then a tram went rattling by and shook me from my reverie. I ran downstairs to where the ladies were washing up after the party tea; and had a good laugh to myself at poor Father Christmas, hunting in all the odd corners for his hat.

Eventually, someone told him that I'd been seen creeping upstairs with it and he chased me for it. We had a good laugh together and he walked with me to the corner of our street. After that, we seemed to meet each other quite a lot, though I knew there'd be hell to pay if Dad found out. Girls at school didn't have young men friends.

Father Christmas called me his little girl in brown, and now all my dreams were centred around him. When I grew up, he would still be waiting for me; and we could get married and he would never ever go to a pub, or swear, or take off his belt to us, his family. We'd have lots of children and take them all to chapel every Sunday and say Grace at mealtimes like they did in the Brown family. Life was going to be wonderful...

Then, Eva found out and told Mum and she put her foot down. "Going around with a man old enough to be your father, I hear," she stormed at me. "Your father will kill you if he finds out. So you'd better put a stop to it, and think a bit harder about school. You'll never get a good report this term!"

As though I cared any more, about school, since I was leaving anyway. Father Christmas wasn't old enough to be my father, in fact he was only about four years older than me, but a nineteen year old who had been at work for five years, certainly seemed a man compared with a fifteen year old schoolgirl. So I cooled off him for a bit, anything to avoid trouble, and I stayed away from the chapel for a time too, never giving any word of explanation and just laughing my way out of it when Father Christmas tried to ask me what was wrong.

All too quickly came the summer, I said goodbye to all my school friends and thought about the big city in which I was to earn a living. There was no question of my going to the underwear factory, for I was hopeless at sewing and hated it anyway, and I couldn't see myself fitting in at the factory where Eva now held an office job.

For a week or so, I moped around at home, but clearly this would not be tolerated. The very air was heavy with reproach when Eva and Gwen put their wages on the table.

"What do you want to do?" asked Mum, perplexed and clearly out of her depth.

"I wanted to go to college and become a teacher, you know that," I replied, "but since I can't, I want to write books."

Mum shook her head and when our insurance man called, she asked him what he thought I ought to do, but he was vague. No office experience, no shorthand, or typing, nothing but an unfinished grammar school education. I could recite 'Gray's Elegy' from beginning to end and back again to the first verse, which I had once done for a bet at school. I knew whole scenes from 'Julius Caesar', and I could fathom out most mathematical problems, but that was all. No good at all in the cut throat world of competition for work.

"What she really needs, is a year at a commercial college," mused the insurance man, but Mum cut in sharply. "She's left school because we can't afford to keep her there, so it's no use making that sort of suggestion and putting ideas in her head."

We bought the newpapers for a few mornings, but nothing came of that and after another week or so, Dad got fed up, as I knew he would.

"Plenty of work around, if you look for it," he said. "Take a penny bus ride and walk through Shoreditch. Lots of vacancies for girls. No need for you to be out of work. It's only men that are not wanted," he finished bitterly.

So we set out, Mum and I, past big box making factories, 'machinists wanted' signs and 'girls to learn upholstery' notices. Everyone wanted girls to use their hands, not brains, and it never occurred to my poor Mum that we were in the wrong area.

At last, we came to Featherstone Street, just off Old Street, and there we stood before a sign. "Girl wanted to make herself useful." The place was a very small printers and bookbinders, and Mum's eyes lit up. "Here you are. You said you wanted to write books. You can learn to make them as well here, and you never know, you might get a chance to write for them as well." I don't think she really believed that herself, but I was fed up by this time and we walked in. It was dark and smelly and I longed to turn and run, but Mum was behind me, pushing me forward towards the seedy looking individual, who was the boss.

So I started in the brave new world of industry for twelve shillings a week. I made cocoa, washed up, ran errands, interleaved pamphlets with newspaper as they came off the printing machine and learned to use a perforating machine. I also had to answer the phone on occasion, just to lie and say "I'm sorry, there's no one here but me. Can I take a message?" while the boss stood breathing heavily down my neck, smelling of beer and smoke.

He was a slippery customer, my bald headed boss, and he was always contriving to get one of the girls alone. After a while, he turned his attentions to me, and he would call me over to the little cubby hole where I made the cocoa, put his sweaty arms around me and kiss me with wet, slobbery lips. "Nice?" he would ask, and, dumb with misery, I would nod my head and wish I could kill him. Sometimes I would see my father passing by, and longed to rush out and tell him, but I was dead scared of losing my job. I dared not throw it up, and was terrified of getting the sack, so I endured weeks of untold misery. When I felt particularly miserable, I would find myself thinking of Father Christmas with his twinkling eyes and curly hair and his kind and gentle manner. It wouldn't be revolting if he kissed me, but he never did.

One morning, old Mr Thorn sent me to Moorgate, to a big block of offices. I wandered along in the bright sunshine, wishing I was one of those lucky people who worked there, when I stopped to look in the windows of the Methodist Book Room. There was an open hymn book on display, and I thought it would be fun to learn the words of the hymn, two verses on the way there and the other two on the way back. Blow old Thorn and his slobbery kisses, if I kept him waiting for his cocoa, that was his hard luck. So I stopped; and tarried even longer on the return journey, hoping that the cocoa would have been made by someone else. But no such luck, and I had once again to endure his sexy passes.

Next week, going again to Moorgate, I went straight to the bookshop window, glad to see that the hymnbook had been changed and another hymn revealed. I began to learn it, and reading it through, stopped dead. Surely...this hymn had been put there for me, especially the second verse.

I thank Thee Lord, that all our joy,
Is touched with pain,
That shadows fall on brightest hours,
That thorns remain,
So that earth's bliss may be our guide, and not our chain.

Well, my Thorn was certainly my cross to bear, my thorn in the flesh, so to speak, but I thought that I'd put up with it long enough and felt that I wasn't called upon to endure it any longer.

I hurried back to the smelly little printers and into the cubby hole to make the cocoa, and when the greasy Mr Thorn came up and put his arms around me, I saw red, came to my senses and did what I should have done long ago. No job was worth this, so I caught him a resounding crack on his bald head with the milk saucepan. To my great surprise, he gave me an injured look, turned and walked away, and from then on he left me severely alone. He turned his unwelcome attentions to another poor kid, and started sending me out on errands on every possible occasion. I rejoiced in my new found freedom, looked in all the shop windows and wandered through the nearby market. I sat in the sunshine in Bunhill fields, close by the tombstone of John Bunyan and thought how silly I had been not to stand up for myself all this time.

I didn't see much of my friend Father Christmas these days, but I couldn't see much future in it. We'd never got any further than holding hands anyway. He had nice hands, nothing much to look at because they were grimed with stencil ink from his work, but they were nice firm dry hands; and if there was one thing I could not stand, it was clammy damp hands. Although I was nearly seventeen now, I had no regular young man as Eva had. I found fault with all the boys I went out with, and the most recent one I had parted from just because of his damp hands!

I had set my sights higher than the boys of Bethnal Green anyway. My latest ambition was to be a minister's wife. Not our minister, since he was happily married, but the wife of any vicar, parson or missionary who'd have me. If I'd been a man, I know I'd have been a preacher; I used to spend hours dreaming up sermons, but since I couldn't, the next best thing was to be the preacher's wife. I was deadly jealous of our minister's wife, because of the life she lived. Presiding over the women's meeting, having the deacons and their wives to tea, giving out the Sunday School prizes and making little speeches, oh, she was a lucky woman.

Problem. How to become a parson's wife if you don't know any parsons. Not even half fledged ones with high hopes. I think I'd have made a bee line for any theological student who swam within my sights, even if he had wet hands and wet kisses, another of my pet hates since my experiences with the dreadful old Thorn. But there it was, all the eligible young men I knew were either shop assistants, printers or postmen, cobblers or carpenters, and though the Lord Himself was a carpenter, I was aiming higher up the social scale, but hadn't a clue as to the rules of the game.

One Sunday evening, Mr Brown, who still watched over me with a Christian and fatherly eye, asked to see me for a moment. He took me into the deacon's vestry and began by ticking me off. I had been chairing our youth club meeting on a wet and thundery evening. Our minister, who was due to come and speak, had sent a message saying his wife was not very well, and as she was dead scared of thunder, he had decided to stay home with her and asked to be excused.

Somehow, this made me spitting mad; and I stood up, gave the young people the message from the minister and then began to read from the Bible, having changed the reading at the last moment. I began, slowly and deliberately, to read the parable of the man who gave a dinner party; and when all was ready, the guests began to make excuses. When I reached 'I have married a wife and therefore I cannot come,' I paused significantly and said, "Excuses, like mankind himself, have not changed over the years."

This caused a terrific burst of applause from the meeting, but someone told Mr Brown and now he took me to task.

"You are altering, Doris," he mourned, "you are not your usual sunny self. Something is wrong. Is it home, or work? Aren't you happy at work?"

Happy? He just had to be joking! I stood looking at him for a moment, then suddenly, out it all tumbled. The horrible old Mr Thorn, the lies on the phone, the aimless wanderings through Whitecross Street and the sheer hopelessness of trying to be anybody, let alone somebody. "We must get you away," he said kindly. "The trouble is, it's hard to find a vacancy, apart from my friend Mr Colston at the factory. But I'll have a think. In the meantime, no more misuse of scripture."

That night, he called to see Mum and Dad. He was tactful and made no mention of the sexy Mr Thorn, but he told them I was doing no good there. Gwen was now earning over a pound a week. She worked an overlock machine on piece work, getting about one and six for overlocking a dozen pairs of knickers. I just couldn't see myself doing this, but there it was. Gwen was getting on and I wasn't.

Happiness didn't enter into it, or satisfaction in work. I knew that even Gwen was not really happy. Admittedly, she loved needlework and was really good at it, but it was designing and the artistry that she loved; and there couldn't be much artistry in overlocking knickers all day long. But the money — there was plenty of artistry in a pound note as far as my family were concerned, and an appointment was made for me to see the great Mr Colston.

In fear and trembling, I went into his office the next day. I wasn't often scared, but I dreaded that he'd see through me, realise that I was hopeless at sewing and didn't want the job anyway. His old father sat in the office with him and smiled at me, such a warm friendly smile that I felt worse than ever, wondering what questions they'd ask me. I couldn't have lied to them, and dreaded their questions.

"Why do you want to leave your present job" was a fairly easy one, and although I kept quiet about the trouble with old Thorn, I told them about the lies and the swearing that went on and the sheer waste of time that I endured. "I just can't work there any longer," I finished.

"Well, you won't find any troubles like that with us, will she father?" smiled Mr Colston, "and although you'll have to start as a learner, I'm sure you'll soon pick it up and be earning as much as your sister."

So I arranged to start the next week, and once the excitement of giving in my notice at the printers was over, I had plenty of time to regret the step I had taken. I was dead sure I'd never even learn to thread the needle of the wretched machine! Gwen was kind and tried to explain all she could about the work, but I couldn't see myself earning one and six a week!

That Sunday night, I prayed for guidance. "Please God, don't let me do the wrong thing," I cried. The last hymn of the service should have been a comfort.

All the way my Saviour leads me,
What have I to ask beside...

finishing with

For I know whate'er befall me,
Jesus doeth all things well.

I suppose it was so, but didn't feel very optimistic when we set off together on the Monday morning. We took a bus to Chancery Lane and walked up to Holborn, this inbred saving of a penny still part of our very being. Chancery Lane was the end of the threepenny journey, and not even on a soaking wet morning would we sport that extra penny to ride up to Kingsway.

I reached the factory and took off my coat, feeling dead scared and bitter about setting out to earn my living doing the only thing I really hated and was absolutely no good at.

Some of the girls said hello, but I could feel their thoughts as their eyes lighted upon me. So this is what comes of going to a posh school and learning all that poetry and stuff and all that German? Finishing up as one of us, but all behind. Doing a fourteen year old job at seventeen! I longed to grab my coat and make a run for it, but then, with a sudden clatter, the machines started up. Gwen grabbed a big pile of peach locknit knickers and threw herself into the making of them, for time was money and at threeha'pence a pair, you just had to get cracking.

I sat there for a bit and then a tall, very nice looking girl came out from the little office and told me that Mr Alan wanted to see me. She took me to his door and gave me a friendly smile as she ushered me in. 'Mr Alan' was the Mr Colston I had seen the previous week. "Doris," he said, crinkling his face into a smile, "I've got a feeling that you aren't very keen on learning to be a machinist." I sat still, wondering whether my face had given me away. Was this kicking out time? But he was smiling so kindly...

"I should think," he went on, "that you are fairly intelligent. You've had a good education, even if it has been cut short, but I gather you can learn pretty quickly. How would you like to start in the office? We need a willing helper there."

Well, now the boot was on the other foot. It was I who felt like kissing, for I could willingly have flung my arms round his neck there and then.

"I didn't say anything the other day," he went on, "because I wasn't quite sure. But I like people who are willing to have a go at anything, and I was glad to see that you were willing to start off as a machinist. So we'll start you as our office junior and see how you get on."

I hardly took in hours or wages – I think I'd have worked for him for nothing, but he cut short my grateful thanks and took me along to the office, where I was delighted to find I'd be under the wing of the girl with the friendly smile.

I took to the work like a duck to water, and my uncanny memory for numbers and figures was a great help. 'Our walking telephone directory', Mr Alan called me and since every garment made in the factory was known by its number, it wasn't long before I could reel off all the numbers that each of the big Knightsbridge and Oxford Street stores bought. Even the buyers got to depend on my knowing what they wanted and since the switchboard was my responsibility, I was soon on first name terms with lots of the assistants in the big stores.

I taught myself to type and although I had no shorthand to begin with, I was soon able to write letters for Mr Alan. What a different life it was!

Apart from one short spell during the war, I stayed with Colstons until my first baby was due, thoroughly enjoying myself and never ceasing to be grateful for the chance which had been given me.

Old Mr Colston was a dear. Whenever he had occasion to tick us off, which wasn't often, he would come up to the office with a clean white hankie in his clenched fist. He'd growl a bit and cast withering scorn upon any error, soon reducing his clerk to tears. Then he would put the hankie into her hand, tell her gruffly to dry her tears, and march out of the room. Later, he would come back, contrite and forgiving. "Doris," he'd say softly, "I'm a bad tempered old man. Put this in your Sunday School box," and he'd leave a ten shilling note on my desk.

I was very keen on the Sunday School nowadays. I had proved so very often in my young life that there was a God, a loving and forgiving God who bothered about the kids of Bethnal Green. I was so sure of this, that I had to make sure that none of the little ones I met up with, would go out in ignorance of this wonderful heavenly care that was theirs for the asking. So I became a Sunday School teacher. It was a far cry from my first ambition to teach, but a very rewarding one.

There was one little girl in my class, who came from what even I called a real slum. She and her three brothers and sisters lived with their parents in a tumbledown house just off Green Street, There were two rooms down and two up, but they let one of the upstairs rooms. The father and the boys slept in the upstairs room and the mother and three little girls slept downstairs. But this division of the sexes didn't prevent new babies from turning up with monotonous regularity, and although I called and duly admired each new baby as it came, I couldn't help wondering why they didn't stop producing.

Perhaps the mother felt this, because on one occasion, she picked up the bundle of wet and whimpering new baby, dropped it into its cot and said, "Ah well, what's coming to yer, comes."

Her husband, an out of work dockie, was a real Micawber and was always expecting something to turn up. Dock work enouraged this attitude to life, being mostly casual labour, but he did nothing to help himself. "One day," he would muse, "one day, things will be different for us. We'll get out of this hole and start fresh. Maybe I'll get a little job what's regular, with a bit coming in each week, so's we know where we are." Yet when he did get a week's work and they invited me to tea on the Sunday, there would be gritty cockles and lurid 'Palace Cake' for tea, the baby had a new silk bonnet and the other children bright straw hats and new caps while their feet were still hanging out of their shoes.

Life did change for them in the end in the dual shape of T.B., which took four of the children, and one of Hitler's bombs which accounted for the rest and for the wretched slum in which they lived.

They were not the only really poor family in the school and my heart ached for some of the children. I used to invite them to our house to tea and Mum would ply them with home made cake and jelly. The National Sunday School Union owned a property in Bournemouth, by the lovely name of House Beautiful and when any of the poor children had been really ill, we would manage to get them away for a fortnight. They wrote glowing letters and hated coming home away from the lovely seaside. "I never knew there was such a big sea," wrote one, "it's so much bigger than Southend." In my heart, I envied these kids I tried so hard to get away, because I had never been any further than Southend myself at that time.

Father Christmas was a Sunday School teacher too, and now I was on first name terms with him. Out of school uniform I seemed to be catching up with him, and now not even my sister could say that he was too old for me. He walked home with me sometimes after teachers' meetings, but I was always elusive about meeting him any other time. He was poor, desperately poor. His job wasn't much and he had a mother to support. His brother, nearly ten years older than he, was married and lived some way away, so that Eric seemed always to be at his mother's beck and call, doing her shopping because she was out at work, or taking her to the market or doing her housework. I'd heard lots about possessive mothers of sons, so I had a further reason for not wasting too much time and thought in his direction.

It was about this time that I became very friendly with a man I'd never met. Colin Edwards was just a voice, though an influential one, in one of the big manufacturers' offices. Colstons bought rolls of silk from his firm, and it was a standing joke that if our stock keeper was told that a material was not available, or temporarily out of stock, I could usually manage to get a delivery for us by phoning Colin Edwards personally. I knew he was a fairly important personage in his office and most people phoning got fobbed off with his secretary, but whenever I rang, I had only to say, "Tell him it's Doris from Colstons," and I was through. We used to chat for ages about all sorts of things; and then one day, when he rang, he asked me if I'd go with him to his company's Sports Day in Kent.

"Bring one of your friends," he suggested, "and I'll bring one of the fellows from the department."

What excitement this caused at the office! It was easy to find one of the girls to accompany me, and we went up to Oxford Street one lunch time to buy new dresses. I even had my very first perm for the occasion. Gosh, what agony to endure for a blind date! Sitting for hours with every hair screwed up to a mass of electric wire, getting hotter and hotter as it baked the hair, and then the wrestling match as the frizz was pulled into some sort of order.

Came the Saturday of the Sports Day, and the weather smiled upon us. Colin and his friend Arthur came to call for us at the office, and Mr Colston met them at the door.

"Now, take care of my girls," he laughed, "and give them a good time."

Good time! I'd never had a time like it. To start with, I'd never been to a restaurant to a meal, apart from the odd snack at Lyons, but Colin and Arthur took us to a big grill room. We had chops, and I recall they had little frills around the bone. The chops were not all that tender, to my way of thinking, and I saw the sense in the old saying, mutton dressed up as lamb.

113

Then came a train journey to Kent and on the way, Colin and I got to know each other quite well. I really liked him, now that we'd met; and he was certainly keen.

"You are funny, you fascinate me," he kept saying. Seems that was his favourite word, because later he said that he'd love his mother to meet me. She'd be fascinated. I bet she would, I thought, when he showed me a photograph of her. Just a snap in the garden, he said it was, and there was this willowy blonde standing by the net of a tennis court, racquet in hand.

"I suppose the tennis court is in your garden," I jeered in my most sarcastic voice, and it was Arthur who answered. "Yes, it is." Just as though there was nothing peculiar in having a whole tennis court in your garden!

Tea time came, and I looked with longing at the lovely cream horns and meringues that were being served; and helped myself to a miserable piece of fruit cake, ordinary as could be. The trouble was, I had spotted the pastry forks and hadn't a clue as to how one ate a cake with a fork. So I left well alone and ate sandwiches instead.

Colin lived in Kent himself, but insisted on getting on the train and coming back to London Bridge with me. We had an empty first class compartment, and no sooner did the train start, than he put his arms around me and began to kiss me as though his life depended on it. It was quite enjoyable too, and I knew I could easily fall for this handsome looking young fellow, with his Oxford accent and his easy and attractive manner.

We reached London Bridge and I tidied my hair and prepared to say cheerio, but he held tight to my hand. "I'll see you right home," he said and I froze in horror.

Imagine Colin Edwards walking down our street, where like as not there'd be a couple of women with babies at the breast standing at the doors, or old men sitting on chairs outside, or small boys watering the gutter. Imagine Colin coming in our house, where Dad would be sat with his greasy cap on his head, whether inside or out in our garden. Tennis court! We had a pigeon loft and a row of stones, and a tin bath hanging up on the wall.

I shook my head. "You don't want to come all the way back with me. You know I live in Bethnal Green." It was common knowledge that Alan Colston got all his staff from the one source.

"Actually, our cook lives in Bethnal Green," laughed Colin. "I've been there once, when she was ill and I ran her home in the car. Please, let me see you home."

I shook my head the harder and ran off, to where a bus was waiting. "I'll phone you on Monday," I called, giving him a wave.

What a weekend I spent! Goodness knows what attracted him to me, but my real image had not ruined the phone image he had built up. Yet... how could he fit in? "Class is class," I had once heard my mother say, and I had laughed at this typical Bethnal Green attitude. Yet to go out with Colin would mean cutting myself off from all the friends I had and all I held dear.

He didn't wait for me to phone on Monday, but rang me early, almost as soon as I reached the office. I hedged when he tried to date me, and when I left at five thirty, there he was, waiting outside the office door. He took me to tea; and I settled for fish and chips...and couldn't go wrong with them. But I was mistaken again, for instead of an ordinary knife and fork, there were special fish ones, with a curly bit at the end of the knife, though whether you used the curly bit or held it uppermost, I just hadn't a clue. So I toyed with the chips until I got a chance to see what someone else was doing, but it was an uncomfortable few minutes.

We saw each other several times after that and I was sorely tempted. But in my heart I knew that I'd never fit in and besides, he just laughed at me for going to church.

"Well, God," I prayed, "you'd better show me what to do, because I really don't know." And on the following Sunday, when the minister announced his text, my ears pricked up at the words of St Paul.

> For I have learned, in whatsoever state I find myself, therewith to be content.

There it was, an answer just for me. I told Colin that I didn't want to go on seeing him, and after a few hopeless meetings, he got the message. The girls thought I was mad.

"Do you know, his Dad's a director of the firm?" said our stock-keeper, shaking his head at my foolishness.

But I couldn't help it. Colin's world and mine could never meet, not in those pre-war days.

Eva's courtship was now reaching a successful conclusion. The ring had been purchased and admired and a flat had been found and suitably furnished. My father had come up trumps and got everything in the furniture line at cost price from a little Jewish cabinet maker in Shoreditch.

"A lovely job," he told Eva, when she went to see what he had to offer. "It breaks me heart to have to part with it at such prices, but times are hard me dear, and I haven't sold a thing this month. Got to pay the rent somehow, and if it wasn't that I wanted to do your father here a favour, I couldn't keep to your prices. I'd get ten times what I'm asking you, from Harrods. Trouble is, they are overstocked at present." It was true too, he did make for Harrods, though of course, he didn't sell to them directly. He made for the big firm that employed my Dad, and they sold to Harrods at a much higher price.

So Eva got her solid oak dining suite, her mahogany and walnut bedroom furniture and all her bits and pieces. Gwen made her curtains and I went over to the flat in Hackney to help get it straight, almost envious of her. She did have some nice things.

She was terribly nervous on her wedding eve, and as always, when nervous, she took it out on us. We couldn't do a thing to please her. "As bridesmaids, you've got to do as I tell you and wait on me," she kept saying and did she keep us running around!

Eventually, we were sent to take her 'going away' clothes to the bridegroom's house, as the wedding reception was being held there. I was all for having a row with her, not being nearly so meek and mild as I had been. I was still smarting a bit from the Colin episode, and all Eva's swanking made me mad. I kept imagining the sort of wedding I might have been having in the future, if I hadn't sent him away. But Gwen was the peacemaker and she tried her hardest to cheer me up. When we came to a small church, half way between our place and the Browns, we stopped and hung Eva's new hat on the railings, dumped her new case on the pavement and sat on a little seat and discussed it all.

"You might just as well keep quiet and put up with it all," said Gwen, philosophically, "because, after tomorrow, she'll be Mrs Brown and she won't be one of us any more. Then she'll only be a visitor when she comes to us, and she won't be able to tick us off or anything."

"Do you reckon she'll have a baby?" I asked. Babies always followed the wedding in our circles, and we sat there contemplating the unlikely idea of Eva as a mother.

Gwen stood up and took the hat off the railings, knocking out the dent with her fist. "Well, we'd better get on. At least, after tonight, we'll have a bedroom each."

The highlight of the wedding, to my mind. A bedroom to myself!

The November wedding day was typical. Gloomy and inclined to be foggy. The atmosphere at home wasn't much brighter, either. Dad was not in a festive mood. The idea of going to church didn't appeal to him in the first place; and the fact that we were going on to Browns afterwards was not exactly his idea of a wedding 'do'.

"I don't know how long we'll be expected to stay with those bloody Bible punchers," he remarked gloomily. He went out with one of the uncles for a quick drink and this put Eva on edge, to say the least. Supposing he didn't come home in time!

But the uncle had been well primed by his wife, and they were not long. When they returned however, Dad heard our voices raised. We were not exactly quarrelling, but arguing rather, over placing of the bridal veil, or the tying of the sashes, or something like that.

"Quarrelling, are you?" he stormed, bursting into the room. "Don't you think I've got enough to put up with today, without you carrying on! I'll kick the three of you up the bloody aisle, that's what I'll do! And when he says 'who giveth this woman?' do you know what I'm going to say? 'Take her, and a bloody good riddance!' You just see if I don't, or I'll swing first!"

We sat, in stunned silence. Dad was capable of anything, we knew that. And if he let us all down...it cast a black cloud of gloom over the remainder of the getting ready.

When we reached the chapel, I was praying like mad. "Oh, please God, don't let him do it. Please God." But I didn't have complete faith in my prayers that day, and although we all walked sedately up the aisle, my heart was pounding like mad when the minister started the service. "Dearly beloved..."

"Who giveth this woman?" he asked, and Dad gestured slightly. I thought everyone must be able to hear the drumbeat that was my heart. "I do," answered Dad, in a meek little voice. So much for his swinging that day!

When we came out of the church, the sun was breaking through and a small knot of onlookers stood outside. Among them, I was amazed to see my Father Christmas, though why he bothered, I couldn't think. Eva certainly didn't invite him to the wedding. As we got into the car and drove away in our pink silk dresses, beautifully made by Gwen, I caught his eye and he gave me a special smile. I knew that he hadn't come to see Eva in all her wedding glory, but just to see me. It was a comforting thought.

There was no honeymoon after the wedding breakfast. November was not exactly seaside weather in England, and the very word 'abroad' was barely in common use at that time. Apart from soldiers and sailors, no one we knew ever went abroad.

So Eva and Jim went off to their flat, and the party, if you could call it that, was soon over. We said our goodbyes to the Browns and I expect the Brown relations were glad to see us go. I know my Dad and uncles were like dogs let off the leash, as soon as we got clear of the house. I'd have rather stayed with the Browns, but Dad and the other men made their way to the Vic and the aunts and Mum went home. By the time they all got home, they were ready to sing 'the old Bull and Bush' and fill up their glasses again and again from the bottles the men brought back. But it was not exactly an exciting wedding.

The very next morning, Gwen and I decided to visit Eva and Jim, little wretches that we were. We couldn't wait to see whether marriage had altered our dear sister. Jim was out, playing the organ, and Eva was cooking the Sunday dinner, beating up the yorkshire pudding and basting the beef, just as Mum did. Then, as we watched, she started to make pastry. Now Gwen was very good at cookery, it had been one of her top subjects at school, and as she watched Eva's valiant efforts, she observed mildly that the pastry was too wet.

"It'll keep sticking to the rolling pin, like that," she finished, as Eva scraped and rolled for the umpteenth time.

Eva wiped her hands without speaking, her face livid with temper. "How dare you, a kid like you, try and teach a married woman how to cook!" She opened her door with a flourish and we ran down the stairs, having a good old giggle as we went. "I bet Jim won't think that tart is just like mother's," I laughed, thinking of Mrs Brown's featherlight pastry.

We were doomed to disappointment about the baby, too. No swelling lump marred the bride's figure and all my fond hopes of having a nice little baby to nurse, were in vain. It was a shame, to my mind, because Eva would probably have had a nice little baby, all beautifully kept and dainty. Actually, it was ten years before that baby put in an appearance, and by that time I was too busy with my own to bother much about Eva's.

Like most brides of her generation, Eva gave up work immediately upon marriage, for every man expected to support his wife. Not many firms accepted married women anyway, so Mum and Eva went out together, shopping in Roman Road, or going to the pictures.

Nothing was ever said now about moving. Frankly, Eva didn't care, and openly referred to our street as a slum. She was living in Hackney, her flat was in a nice clean house as big as yer aunts, and her husband had a nice clean job in the piano world. I felt sometimes that life was a bit hard, because maybe, if we had lived somewhere decent, I might have dared to take Colin home, and who knows what might have followed?

Yet now I know so much more. Colin joined the R.A.F. at the outbreak of war; and he was one of the few whom the many mourned. I'd have been a war widow, and then what would have happened, had I cut myself adrift from my folks? A pretty bleak and lonely outlook, it would have been.

During the following September, came an event which changed everything for me, and it was brought about indirectly by Oswald Moseley's Blackshirts. They had been troublesome all summer, holding meetings in

Victoria Park and marching through Grove Road. But this particular Sunday, they had a near riot right outside our chapel, just as the children were leaving Sunday School. Most of them ran through the back streets and some of the parents called to take their offspring home, but we were left, Father Christmas and I, with a handful of little girls. They were too scared to set foot outside, and frankly, so was I. There were police whistles and scuffles, and surging mobs of angry men, throwing stones and jumping off the steps of our building.

Time went on and the whitefaced children began to weep.

"Come on," said Father Christmas finally, "let's wait our opportunity and make a run for it. If we go through to the back of the church and down the little side steps, we can make it, if we are quick."

So we took the children's hands and made our way to the back steps. When the crowd thinned momentarily, having boarded a tram they had got off the lines, we made a dash and were soon safe in the small street behind Grove Road. We took the children home, seeing each safely to their door, and breathed a sigh of relief.

"Thank God for that," I said, turning to him with a smile.

"Now I've got to see you safely home," he answered, taking my hand.

It was as though a light had suddenly shone through the grey of my day. How right, how very right, it seemed, to be walking along hand in hand with him, and I knew, at that very moment, that this was the way I wanted to walk, for the rest of my life. All my dreams about meeting the embryo parson went up in smoke, all my vague ideas of being swept away against my better judgement by the glamorous Colin just vanished into thin air; and all my plans about being rich and famous, just disappeared. Now I knew exactly what I wanted and my feet were firmly on the path. My Beloved, my Eric, was a real Christian, a man who lived for God and to whom God meant everything, and I wanted nothing more than to share his life, however tough and humble it might be.

That night, as I sank into my bed, my new dream was born. Maybe, some day, I would be a minister's mother. With such a man as mine, our children could not grow up any other way than with a faith.

Some years later, when our first son was born, our minister came into the hospital to see me. He stood looking at the little black haired, red faced, day old baby.

"He'd make a lovely little parson," he laughed," and that pair of lungs would stand him in good stead." I picked up the screaming little bundle and held him to me.

"Perhaps, some day, he will be," I replied slowly, "but I'd never wish him to enter the church because his mother wanted him to. It would have to be of his very own free will, so I'll never ever suggest it."

So I kept my secret dream in my heart, and when it was realised and I saw my beloved son ordained, my gratitude to the Almighty was too deep for words.

Ten

Bethnal Green was beginning to alter now. Some of the worst slums were being pulled down, and the overcrowding was much less severe. People were beginning to accept the new estate at Dagenham, and it was a fairly simple matter to ask for a house there and get allocated one within a few weeks or months.

Steve married and moved out there, and to see him so houseproud with his pretty little wife was almost funny, when I thought about the way we used to turn his Mum's house upsidedown playing games!

Some of the Sunday School children moved out too and Eric and I used to go visiting them. There was a lot of foolish talk about Bethnal Green people keeping coals in the posh new bathrooms, but I never met anyone who ever did, or even knew of anyone who did! As I knew them, removal from the narrow streets broadened their horizons in more than one way, and they tried hard to live up to their clean and decent surroundings. They bought new furniture and new curtains, and even put carpets on the floors. They saved hard and got what they wanted, and you could furnish a little place nicely for a hundred pounds then.

Not everyone went to council estates though, when they moved from the Green. For they were building hundreds and hundreds of little houses for sale, all around Woodford and Ilford and Barkingside. Eric and I would go out and look at them sometimes on a Saturday afternoon, though any chance we had of saving for the deposit on one, was very remote.

Eric's mother was a cantankerous old woman. She hated me with all the proverbial hatred of the mother-in-law and tried her hardest to make sure I didn't get my hands on her son. A mystery surrounded his father, and I was determined to get to the bottom of it, for Eric had never known him and could find no trace of him having died.

"Your brother must remember him, even if you don't," I said one day, when we were discussing it. After all he was ten years older than Eric. "Why don't you ask him?"

My easy going fiance wasn't very keen on this idea though.

"Why dig up the past?" he argued.

I nearly exploded at that. "Why? because I must know, that's why. Supposing your father is a raving lunatic, or something like that. It might be hereditary, and then where shall we be?"

I could see all my dream children fading into the realm of never never, and, much as I loved Eric, I wanted that family badly.

So eventually, he asked his mother, but, grown man that he was, she clouted him over the head and threatened him with a knife. "I knew it would mean trouble," he said, rubbing the bump on his head.

"Think," I said finally. "What can you remember? Can you ever remember any man coming to the house or anything?"

"No," he answered. "My mother always worked as an office cleaner, for as long as I can remember. She was always at the same big office block in the City. On Saturdays, she used to take me with her, and when I was small, I used to sit in the boss's big chair and watch her working. Sometimes, the boss was in the building, and he'd come in, pat me on the head and give me a sixpence. About the only time I ever had any money," he laughed ruefully.

On schooldays he would come home and go across the street to wait at his Gran's until his mother returned from work. "My Gran didn't like me much, he mused. She would never light the gas for me, and I had to sit in the firelight until my uncle came home from work. He wasn't married, and Gran and my auntie idolised him. Once he came home, the light was lit, the tea was made and the fire poked up into a blaze. That's why Mum dislikes you so. She thinks I should be like my uncle, and take over our household, now that I'm working. She doesn't think I should marry."

"Well, that's one blessing," I said. "If there was any reason why we shouldn't marry, she'd have been quick enough to tell you."

At last, we sent for a copy of the birth certificate. The blank spaces where father's name should be told their tale; and in those days, when the stigma of illegitimacy was visited on the children as well as the sinning parents, I knew that there'd be hell to pay if I told my parents. So we let them go on thinking that his mother was a widow. But who was father? And why the ten year gap between the sons? Were they two separate follies, or was it a long affair?

Eventually, we went to see Eric's brother, who was not at all keen to have his family secrets hauled out in front of his wife. So he took Eric off for a long walk; and it was not until we were in the bus on the way home that my curiosity was satisfied.

Eric had looked so utterly dumbfounded, that I knew he had news. "Well?" I asked impatiently.

"You know that boss of my Mum's? The one I told you about, who used to pat me on the head and give me a sixpence? He was my father!" I was absolutely astounded. "Him! Your Mum must have been stark staring crazy. What did she get out of it? What, I ask you?"

Eric shrugged his shoulders and started to laugh. "Not even hot water to scrub the floors! She was always moaning about the cold water. I saw his wife and daughter once," he went on. "They called in at the office, wearing fur coats, and they drove off in a big car."

"Where is he now?"

"Dead." I was sorry about that. I had a crazy idea about forcing him, blackmailing him even, into making the stupid woman an allowance to get her off our back, but it wasn't to be.

"Well," I said finally, "at least, you're a gentleman's son. On your father's side you're no cockney. Freemen of the City of London, big wigs and businessmen, they're your ancestors, wedding ring or no wedding ring."

It was early in 1937, that I came home from work to find my Mum in a state of deepest gloom.

"I don't know what your father will say," she said, "but we've had the sanitary man round today, with a council surveyor."

"Well, we've had them before, so I suppose we'll get over it," I answered, but I could understand her gloom.

Whenever the sanitary man had called and decided that repairs were urgent, he would send the landlord a letter, telling him what had to be done. The landlord would keep on putting off the work until faced with a summons. Then he would send an odd job man, whom Dad invariably referred to as a bloody old bodger, and he would start the work. Then he'd go off and start a similar job elsewhere, just to keep the authorities happy that the work was in hand. We had known them remove a broken gutter and leave us without one for two months, so that the rain poured down the walls and made them damp, and on one occasion, they had gone up to repair a leaking roof, spent an hour up there and then gone away. Next time it rained, instead of making a wet patch on the ceiling as it had been doing, the rain poured in. Unfortunately, it always seemed to happen in my parent's bedroom, and many a night I've heard them get up, with Dad swearing like mad, to catch the rain in bowls and buckets. Yet he would not hear of moving. He'd given up keeping pigeons when finances were tight, so he no longer had this excuse.

We had always done our own wallpapering and painting, keeping the place looking nice, but often the best handiwork was ruined by the rain coming in. For years after I was married, even living miles away from

Bethnal Green, a heavy rainstorm would send me sneaking upstairs, wherever we lived, just to make sure the rain was not coming in.

Anyway, on this occasion, Mum was more gloomy than usual. Not only had the sanitary man found the usual odd jobs, but the surveyor had condemned the whole front wall of the house. It would all have to come out and be rebuilt, right down to the bottom window sill. It was dangerous and would collapse if left, so needed to be done right away.

It was a couple of days before she dared tell Dad. "The bloody hell they won't pull down my wall," he shouted, "I'll swing first. You let any bloody workman in here to start such larks, and out you go!"

I felt like pointing out that the workman might not need to come in to start pulling down an outside wall, but thought better of it. It was still easier to keep quiet when Dad was having his say.

The weeks went by and nothing happened. It was pretty certain that the landlord, tight fisted cuss that Dad called him, would not do anything until he had to. He was supposed to pay our rates, but never did. We used to get a summons for not paying them and had to take our rent to the court every week until they were paid, getting our rent book marked at the court. So we guessed the old man wouldn't do anything if he thought he could get away with it.

At last, when the tension at home had died down and we thought the whole matter had been forgotten, I came home one day to see scaffolding outside our house and next door.

Dad came home, went out again and got rip roaring drunk. He came home late that night, kicked the poor dog and did his nut generally, threatening to stay home from work to stop the men from pulling the wall down. I offered to move into Gwen's room and let them have mine until the front was finished, but surprisingly, Mum said no.

Next day, the wall was half down, and a tarpaulin draped across the room, but still Mum left the bed there and said that was where they'd sleep.

"Let the silly old bugger put up with it," she said bitterly. "The times I've asked him to move and he's refused. I'm alright, but it won't do his chest much good, with all that cold night air and dust. Let him suffer."

That night, Dad came home in a resigned mood. "It might only take a few days," he said optimistically. Apparently he'd been talking to a fellow at work who'd had a similar experience. "Should be straight by the end of the week."

Dad should have known better. At least, after all those years, he should have known our landlord. Having shown the work was under way, the workmen didn't turn up the next morning, or the next, and the whole of the following week brought no change.

Thick gloom descended on the household. I hadn't known it so quiet since Rosie died. Yet somehow, Mum was different. There was an undercurrent of excitement about her all the time and she seemed the least upset of us all.

The next Saturday, I came in from work and felt her excitement bubbling over.

"This is your father's last chance," she said. "I've found a place this morning. I should have done this years ago."

When Dad came in, she smacked his dinner down in front of him in a most unusual off hand manner.

"No workmen, of course," she said starkly, actually putting the cat among the pigeons.

"What the hell do they care?" moaned my father. "We can all die with pneumonia."

"You can. We won't," replied Mum quickly, then before he had a chance to start roaring at her, she continued, "I've found a place. Eat up your dinner Joe, do. Then you can all get your coats on and come with me. We are going to Leytonstone, and once you've seen it, Joe, you'll change your mind."

We all looked at her in amazement. She hardly ever called him anything but Dad, and this Joe business was in itself unusual.

"I'm not putting my name to any documents," he roared. "I'm not signing all my money away for the next twenty years."

"No one's asking you to. It's a flat," retorted Mum.

"I'm not living upstairs in anyone's house," yelled Dad again, but it seemed to me that the roaring was less vehement than usual.

"It's not upstairs anywhere," said Mum quietly, in the same matter of fact tone. "It's a ground floor flat, and the people upstairs are not our lodgers. It's a divided house, and the garden is ours."

Then she delivered her bombshell, that she should have used years before.

"If you don't want to come Joe, you can stay in this hole by yourself. The girls and I are going, anyway."

I just couldn't believe it, I just couldn't. He put on his coat, paid all our bus fares, and took Mum's arm as we walked through one of the nicest roads in Leytonstone, and Leytonstone, in those pre-war days, was one of the nicest suburbs of East London.

The new landlord was waiting for us at the house. A fine old house, with a long front garden and a big square hall, bigger than yer aunt's. A huge kitchen, bathroom, hot water system and french doors leading out to a pleasant garden.

"Only snag," sighed Mum happily, "you two girls will have to share a bedroom. Will you mind that?"

Would we mind! We just could not believe it.

Dad came in from the garden, whistling happily to himself.

"I'll have to buy a lawn mower, that's for certain. The furniture will look a darn sight better here than it did in the old place."

'Darn sight?' What had happened to the everlasting 'bloody?' I could hardly believe my ears.

Everything was signed and we arranged to move in the following week. Dad walked about on air, looking out seed boxes, repolishing scratches on the furniture, acting all the time as though the whole thing had been his idea. But we didn't care. We were going and that was all that mattered.

On the following Friday morning, I set out as usual for the bus stop, looking back at the poor old house with its tumbling walls for the last time, and mused all the way to work on what had happened there.

"Gosh, I could write a book about it all!"

I went home that night, home on the train to Leytonstone, to home where Mum, busy and happy all day, had already got everything straight and waiting for us.

Lovely Leytonstone...and Goodbye, dear old Bethnal Green.

Stepney Books aims to encourage the writing and publishing of local working people's experiences. To date, we have produced six local histories. *Children of the Green* is the seventh.

Stepney Books is a member of the Federation of Worker Writers and Community Publishers, a growing national movement. Local readers of this book who are interested in joining a writer's group, should contact:

> THAP Writer's Group
> 178 Whitechapel Road, London E1

> Basement Writers
> The Basement, St George's Town Hall, Cable Street, London E1

> Hackney Worker Writers
> Centerprise, 136 Kingsland High Street, London E8

For groups in other parts of the country, contact:

> Federation of Worker Writers and Community Publishers
> c/o 76 Carysfort Road, London N16

Other Stepney Books publications

Victoria Park a social history of East London, by Charles Poulson (in conjunction with Journeyman Press) £1.20

Memories of Old Poplar by John Blake 40p

Under Oars by Harry Harris (in conjunction with Centerprise Publications) 75p

Tough Annie, From Suffragette to Stepney Councillor, Annie Barnes in conversation with Kate Harding and Caroline Gibbs ... £1.50

All titles available from 19 Tomlins Grove, Bow, London E3. Postage extra.

Also *Writing* £1.00 — an anthology of working class writing; and *Voices*, a quarterly anthology of working class writing, published by The Federation of Worker Writers.

Other books about Bethnal Green available from
THAP Bookshop, 178 Whitechapel Road, London E1.

The Photographs of Bethnal Green 1949-1952 by Nigel Henderson £1.50

The Green by A.J. Robinson and D.H.B. Chesshyre £1.00

Also *Writing* £1.00 — an anthology of working class writing; and *Voices*, a quarterly anthology of working class writing, published by The Federation of Worker Writers.